PATIENT
EDUCATION
IN HOME CARE

A Practical Guide
to Effective Teaching
and Documentation

Janet E. Jackson, RN, MS
Assistant Professor
University of Arkansas
Fayetteville, Arkansas

Elizabeth A. Johnson, BSN, CNA
Executive Director
Regional Health Systems, Inc.
Muskogee, Oklahoma

AN ASPEN PUBLICATION®
Aspen Publishers, Inc.
Rockville, Maryland
Royal Tunbridge Wells
1988

Library of Congress Cataloging-in-Publication Data.

Jackson, Janet E.
Patient education in home care: a practical guide to effective teaching and
documentation/Janet E. Jackson, Elizabeth A. Johnson.
p. cm.

"An Aspen publication."
Includes bibliographies and index.
ISBN: 0-87189-769-5
1. Home nursing. 2. Patient education. 3. Self-care, Health-study and teaching.
I. Johnson, Elizabeth A. (Elizabeth Ann), 1952- . II. Title
RT120.H65J33   1988
610.73'43--dc19   88-3391
CIP

Editorial Services: Ruth Bloom

Library of Congress Catalog Card Number: 88-3391
ISBN: 0-87189-874-8

Printed in the United States of America

1 2 3 4 5

To our families and friends for their encouragement and support and to Shelli Hopkins for her enthusiasm and hard work in typing the manuscript.

Janet E. Jackson
Elizabeth A. Johnson

Table of Contents

Preface

The purpose of this book is to provide health care professionals with a practical, workable, and effective handbook that will assist them in teaching self-care to patients and significant others regardless of their educational, social, economic, or cultural background. We as professional nurses with extensive home care experience, both in the Medicare-certified home health agency and private duty nursing areas of home care, have identified with other home care professionals the underutilization of patient teaching.

In reality, patient teaching probably is not underutilized but underdocumented. We believe this text will be a valuable reference to nurses, discharge planners, nursing educators, and nursing students, as well as to other health care professionals who have the ultimate responsibility of caring for and teaching the patient in their home. This book addresses the problems health care professionals face and offers practical and effective methods in assessing the patients' learning needs, developing teaching plans, implementing a system and individualized teaching plan, and then incorporating the teaching plan into the clinical record through comprehensive documentation.

It is also our intent to provide the Medicare-certified home health agency staff with a better understanding of the Medicare regulations governing reimbursement for services rendered. Patient teaching is one of the three skilled components of the Medicare home health benefit.

Because it has been identified as the most underutilized component, it is addressed almost exclusively in this text.

Private insurance companies usually follow Medicare's lead in implementing coverage criteria; therefore, if health care professionals familiarize themselves with Medicare regulations and requirements, it will enable the health care professional who does not routinely deal with Medicare to ensure coverage compliance with other third party payors.

It is our expectation that the text will be used by health care professionals in providing better education for patients in their home. Patient teaching allows patients to possess an increased awareness and understanding of their illness and better coping mechanisms for dealing with acute or chronic conditions. Through this understanding and knowledge, patients will be able to attain an optimum level of health.

For ease of writing, the health care professional addressed in this text is the nurse. Any health care professional should be able to use the first six chapters of this text to assess, plan, implement, evaluate, and document patient teaching in his or her particular area of expertise.

For ease in reading, nurses are referred to using the female gender, and patients are referred to using the male gender. This usage is in no way meant to indicate sexual bias.

Part I

Patient Teaching in the Home Care Setting

The following chapters are intended to assist the health care professional to review principles of patient teaching, examine the teaching/learning process, and recognize barriers, problems, and mistakes in patient teaching. Chapter 1 presents an overview of the principles of patient teaching; Chapter 2 compares the teaching/learning process with the nursing process; and Chapter 3 provides an explanation of common barriers, problems, and mistakes encountered when providing patient teaching, with possible solutions.

These chapters provide a background for assessing patients in the home and developing a teaching plan. Through a thorough understanding of the principles of patient teaching and the teaching/learning process, the health care professional can assess, diagnose, plan, implement, and evaluate the teaching that patients require in the home setting.

Chapter 1

Principles of Patient Teaching: An Overview

Objectives

- To define teaching, learning, and patient teaching with discussion of differences.
- To review the development of patient teaching throughout history.
- To examine the legal implications of patient teaching in the home setting.
- To explore the patient's right to patient teaching.
- To explain the principles of patient teaching including cue identification, goals of patient teaching, guidelines for adult education, and theories and models related to patient education.
- To describe the role of the nurse in patient education.

1

Nurses are not only asked but are expected to do patient teaching in their daily practice, be it an acute care setting, ambulatory care center, physician's clinic, home health agency, or any area of practice. In home health, more than in many other areas of nursing, the nurse is held responsible and accountable for patient teaching. Patient teaching is one of the three components of what Medicare considers skilled nursing. Nurses in home health currently find themselves in an era when cost containment, not access to service, is a major policy trend.[1] Nurses must clearly define and document their role in the delivery of nursing care. Since nurses are expected to teach patients in home health, they must have a clear understanding of the teaching/learning process and the vital role they play.

Although nurses should be teaching, the sad fact remains that often patients are not taught. Magill et al. stated: "Frequently, the reason that patients aren't taught is that nurses lack the knowledge and skills necessary to teach. Lacking the ability they cannot perform the task."[2]

This text hopes to provide nurses with information and materials that will allow them to review knowledge concerning patient teaching and/or develop a knowledge base to assist them in providing patient teaching in home care. It should be a manual that will aid in providing the best possible patient teaching and in documenting the skilled nursing service rendered.

TEACHING AND LEARNING

The literature abounds with definitions of what teaching and learning are. The nurse, in her own mind, must develop her own definitions and beliefs about the teaching/learning process but must first acknowledge what the experts define as teaching and learning.

Chatham and Knapp[3] define teaching as a process that facilitates learning, while learning is thought to have occurred when there is a resultant behavior change. Others[4-6] define teaching as activities by which the teacher helps the student learn, the process of facilitating learning, and a deliberate action that is undertaken to help another person learn to do something. Learning is said to have occurred when a person becomes capable of doing something he or she could not do before. To take it one step further, the person who has learned will be able to explain, discuss, demonstrate, or make something by using a set of ideas.[7]

Patient teaching is much more than what the definitions imply. Duffy and Rankin[8] describe patient teaching as an act in which the nurse becomes involved in assisting her patients to become active members of the health care team and assists them to make informed choices regarding the quality of their life. It also enables the patient to learn things that may help him live a longer and/or fuller life. It should help him learn to reach an optimal level of health.[9]

Nurses must realize that patients learn from them day in and day out. Every time nurses are with their patients, there are opportunities for patient teaching. Nurses must recognize these opportunities and assess the patient's and/or family's need for education, which will be discussed at length in Chapter 2.

HISTORY, LEGAL ISSUES, AND PATIENT RIGHTS

As our society becomes an increasingly educated group of people, the value placed on health, the right to health care, and the right to know how to attain better health has risen greatly. Even though some futurists have indicated that we are moving from an industrial society to an information society, nurses were providing patient teaching to their patients as early as the mid–nineteenth century. It was the visiting nurses who were the most responsible for early patient teaching in both England and the

United States. These nurses recognized the need for health teaching as they became involved in caring for patients in their homes.

As early as 1918, the National League of Nursing stated the need to cover preventative and educational factors for visiting nurses in nursing schools' curricula. Although the incorporation of the principles of teaching and learning has been slow, they are now found in most nursing curricula.

Nurse practice acts have been developed in all fifty states. Their purpose is to protect the lay public from incompetent practitioners through establishing licensing procedures. The law also defines the practice of nursing. Although many of the acts do not clearly define the practice of nursing, many do so specifically. Many acts include the nurse's involvement in patient teaching as part of the practice of nursing. So not only are nurses expected to do patient teaching, many are mandated to do so by law. All nurses should be familiar with the nurse practice act in their state.

"Patient and family teaching must be recorded and is central to adequate and good nursing care in the home."[10] This statement was taken from a list of seven legalities in home care identified by Creighton. She stated that the home health nurse cannot assume that patient teaching was carried out in the hospital. Often, home health nurses must reteach what was taught in the hospital. It is imperative that home health nurses be in close communication with the hospital teaching team to ensure pertinent teaching upon discharge to the home.

In 1975, the American Hospital Association wrote and adopted "A Patient's Bill of Rights." In this document, many areas in patient teaching are covered. The patient has a right to knowledge concerning his condition, the health care delivery system, the immediate environment, and skills needed to care for himself. The goal of this document was to ensure high-quality care that would provide greater satisfaction for the patient, health care providers, and hospitals. Although written for the hospital, these rights carry over, even more so, into the patient's home. All patients have the right to acquire knowledge and skills that will allow them to function at an optimal level of health despite the limitations or restrictions of their current condition.

History shows that nurses have been involved in patient teaching for many years. Current laws mandate that patient teaching be an integral part of practice. It is clear that the public firmly believes they have a right to patient teaching. As a health care worker, patient teaching should be an obligation that nurses strive to fulfill on a daily basis.

GENERAL PRINCIPLES OF PATIENT TEACHING

The following presents general principles of patient teaching to be used in everyday practice. Nurses recognize certain cues from the patient that indicate his need to learn. When nurses respond to that cue, they are teaching. Teaching may be brief or complex: it may take a short time or many days to complete. Patient teaching requires great involvement by both the nurse and patient. The teaching nurse's duty is multifaceted and encompasses many areas.

The goals of patient teaching are

- teaching to promote health
- teaching to prevent illness
- teaching to cope with illness.[11]

It also involves setting goals that will help the patient learn to live life in the healthiest way possible. To reach the goals of patient teaching, the nurse must first understand the principles of patient teaching, some of which include

- Learning is more effective when it is a response to a felt need of the learner.
- Active participation on the part of the learner is essential if learning is to take place.
- Learning is made easier when the material to be learned is related to what the learner already knows.
- Learning is facilitated when the material to be learned is meaningful to the learner.
- Learning is retained longer when it is put into immediate use than when its application is delayed.
- Periodic plateaus occur in learning.
- Learning must be reinforced.
- Learning is made easier when the learner is aware of his or her progress.[12]

The nurse must also look closely at the patient and significant others, who are often responsible for patient care. The majority of these people are adults. Adults bring with them to educational activities different self-images, experiences, and goals. Knowles,[13] considered the father of adult education, offers the following guidelines when teaching adults:

- Adults prefer learning activities based on active involvement and the problems they encounter in their everyday work environment.
- Adults tend to withdraw from learning situations that are potentially humiliating and detrimental to their self-concept.
- Adults possess a large reservoir of life and work experiences and desire opportunities to capitalize on and share their knowledge.
- Adults possess a variety of individual learning styles and rates.
- Adults have many compelling and conflicting demands on their time and thought processes.

Many of these principles and guidelines were derived from various theories and models. Though there are many models and theories used in discussing the teaching/learning process, the following three will be discussed as they relate directly to health teaching: (1) Maslow's Hierarchy of Needs, (2) the PRECEDE model, and (3) the Health Belief model.

Abraham Maslow stated that human beings are dominated by a number of basic needs, and that the lower needs must be met before the higher needs can be met. The needs he identified are

- physiologic
- safety and security
- love and belongingness
- self-esteem
- self-actualization (Figure 1-1).

Maslow believed that human motivation stemmed from man's attempt to meet these needs.

The nurse often focuses on reinforcing or changing a patient's attitudes, perceptions, and/or beliefs about his illness. For change to occur, the patient must usually be motivated. It is understandable, then, how this theory can be helpful in recognizing the patient's needs and his motivation to learn. Narrow[14] stated that Maslow's hierarchy is helpful in assessing the patient and planning educational activities. It can also be helpful in understanding the patient's response or lack of response. She

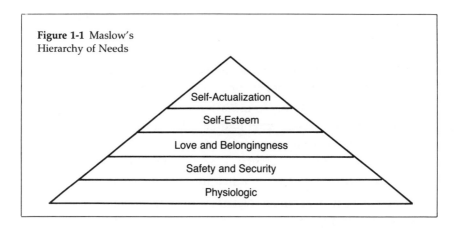

Figure 1-1 Maslow's Hierarchy of Needs

Self-Actualization

Self-Esteem

Love and Belongingness

Safety and Security

Physiologic

indicates that the nurse must be able to recognize signs and symptoms that might indicate unmet needs and must be able to determine how the unmet need might affect the teaching/learning process.

The PRECEDE model is a health education planning model. "PRECEDE" is an acronym for predisposing, reinforcing, and enabling causes in educational diagnosis and evaluation (Table 1-1). This model was developed by Green,[15] who found that there are certain factors in one's environment that influence one's motivation to exhibit certain health behaviors. The model works using a process in which one considers the desired outcomes and works back to the original cause. The model is carried out in the following seven steps:

1. Consider the quality of life.
2. Identify specific health problems and choose the one deserving the most attention.
3. Identify specific health-related behaviors that appear to be linked to the health problem.
4. Categorize factors that have direct impact on the behavior selected:

   - *predisposing factors:* attitudes, beliefs, values, and perceptions that may facilitate or hinder motivation
   - *enabling factors:* barriers created by outside forces
   - *reinforcing factors:* related to feedback that the learner receives from others, be it positive or negative.

5. Decide which factors will be the focus of the intervention.

Table 1-1 The PRECEDE Model

Phase 6	Phases 4-5	Phase 3	Phases 1-2
Administrative diagnosis	Educational diagnosis	Behavioral diagnosis	Epidemiological and social diagnosis
Health education components of health program	Predisposing factors Enabling factors Reinforcing factors	Nonbehavioral causes	Nonhealth factors
		Health problems	Quality of life
		Behavioral causes	

Source: Reprinted from *Health Education Planning: A Diagnostic Approach* by L.W. Green with permission from Mayfield Publishing Company, © 1980.

6. Select interventions and assess problems that may arise.
7. Evaluate.[16]

The Health Belief model (Figure 1-2) was developed by Becker[17] and is probably the most complete theory regarding readiness to take health action. The Health Belief model consists of five elements:

1. *health motivation:* includes the patient's degree of interest in and concern about health matters
2. *susceptibility:* patient perceives himself as vulnerable to the illness and accepts the diagnosis
3. *severity:* how the patient perceives the severity of the illness
4. *benefits and costs:* patient evaluates the value of the regimen in terms of efficacy in decreasing the susceptibility or severity of the illness weighed against the barriers that may be involved in following the regimen
5. *cue to action:* something that arouses these perceptions and increases the likelihood of compliance.

These theories are evidence of the work that has been done in human behavior and the relations between motivation and the learning process. It is evident that the nurse could teach on a daily basis, but if the patient is not motivated to learn or change behavior, little will be accomplished. (Motivation will be discussed in detail in Chapters 2 and 3.) From this information, the nurse can build her knowledge base of teaching and learning and incorporate these principles into her daily practice.

Figure 1-2 The Health Belief Model

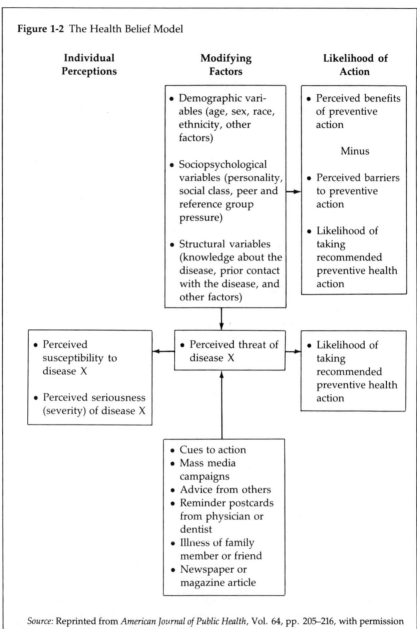

Source: Reprinted from *American Journal of Public Health,* Vol. 64, pp. 205–216, with permission of American Public Health Association, © 1974.

THE ROLE OF THE NURSE

The nurse is the primary source of patient teaching. The reasons for this are the nurse's knowledge, opportunities for patient teaching, and the nature of the patient-nurse relationship. Many physicians indicate that their patients will confide their learning needs to the nurse before talking with them. Knowledge, skill, and caring are attributes of the nurse that allow her to take on the role of teacher. To some, teaching is considered one of the most critical of all nursing interventions.

When teaching, the nurse must strive to teach in such a way that the patient does those things that will contribute to his well-being. Prerequisites to nurse teaching include acquiring essential knowledge, developing skills in teaching, and exploring with the patient what his condition means to him and what plans need to be made. The last of these prerequisites allows the nurse to use her skills in the nursing process to assess, plan, intervene, and evaluate the teaching plan for her patient. (The nursing process is discussed in detail in Chapter 2.)

As the nurse uses her knowledge of teaching/learning principles, she should consider the following questions:

- What factors influence readiness to learn?
- Does the patient want to learn?
- How important is it that the patient learn?
- What should the patient learn?
- What does the patient want to learn?
- What is the best way to teach?
- What can you do to increase the likelihood that your patient will learn whatever you teach?
- How can you tell when a person has learned something?

These questions and many more will be answered in subsequent chapters.

The nurse must also be very active in the coordination of patient teaching activities. In home health, the nurse can organize the teaching activities of all health team members to ensure that duplication of teaching does not occur and that all members reinforce the teaching being done.

With knowledge of the principles, recognition of the need, and acceptance of the obligation of patient teaching, the nurse will incorporate patient teaching into her daily practice. Patient teaching is an integral component of the role of the nurse in home health care.

NOTES

1. M. Auerback, "Changes in Home Health Care Delivery," *Nursing Outlook* 33, no. 6 (November/December 1985):290–291.

2. K. Magill, S. Williams, and A. Caspi, "Patient Education: Progress and Problems," *Nursing Management* 17, no. 2 (February 1986):45.

3. M. Chatham and L. Knapp, *Patient Education Handbook* (Bowie, Md.: Robert J. Brady Co., 1982).

4. B.K. Redman, *The Process of Patient Education*, 5th ed. (St. Louis: C.V. Mosby Co., 1984).

5. B.W. Narrow, *Patient Teaching in Nursing Practice* (New York: John Wiley & Sons, 1979).

6. Ibid.

7. Ibid.

8. K. Duffy and S. Rankin, *Patient Education: Issues, Principles, and Guidelines* (Philadelphia: J.B. Lippincott Co., 1983).

9. Narrow, *Patient Teaching*.

10. H. Creighton, "Legal Implication of Home Health Care," *Nursing Management* 18, no. 2 (February 1987):14–17.

11. Narrow, *Patient Teaching*.

12. B. Dugas, *Introduction to Patient Care*, 2nd ed. (Philadelphia: W.B. Saunders Co., 1972), pp. 214–216.

13. M. Knowles, *The Adult Learner: A Neglected Species*, 2nd ed. (Houston: Gulf Publishing Co., 1978).

14. Narrow, *Patient Teaching*.

15. L. Green, *Health Education Planning: A Diagnostic Approach* (Palo Alto, Calif.: Mayfield Publishing Co., 1980).

16. Redman, *Process of Patient Education*.

17. M.H. Becker, *The Health Belief Model and Personal Health Behavior Health Education Monographs* 2 (1974):326–473.

BIBLIOGRAPHY

Becker, M.H. *The Health Belief Model and Personal Health Behavior. Health Education Monographs* 2 (1974):326–473.

Cross, K. *Adults as Learners.* San Francisco: Jossey-Bass Publishers, Inc., 1981.

Falvo, D. *Effective Patient Education.* Rockville, Md.: Aspen Publishers, Inc., 1985.

Green, L. *Health Education Planning: A Diagnostic Approach.* Palo Alto, Calif.: Mayfield Publishing Co., 1980.

Megenity, J.S., and Megenity, J. *Patient Teaching: Theories, Techniques, and Strategies*. Bowie, Md.: Robert J. Brady Co., 1982.

Stanton, M. "Patient and Health Education: Lessons from the Marketplace." *Nursing Management* 16, no. 4 (April 1985):26–30.

Stanton, M. "Teaching Patients: Some Basic Lessons for Nurse Educators." *Nursing Management* 16, no. 8 (October 1985):59–62.

Chapter 2

The Teaching/Learning Process

Objectives

- To relate the teaching/learning process to the nursing process.
- To describe the assessments made in relation to the learner, the teaching situation, and the teacher.
- To utilize nursing diagnosis when identifying the teaching need.
- To discuss the planning of patient teaching including the establishment of learning objectives and choices of teaching methods.
- To identify guidelines that assist in the implementation of the teaching plan.
- To explore various methods of evaluating the effectiveness of teaching and need for re-teaching when necessary.

2

TEACHING AND THE NURSING PROCESS

In Chapter 1, many general concepts of patient teaching were discussed. The nurse was, we hope, reminded of roles and responsibilities related to teaching. Many times it was stated that patient teaching is an integral part of nursing practice. How does one incorporate patient teaching into daily practice? The nursing process, which is the foundation of nursing practice, is the framework in which a nurse can develop, plan, and carry out teaching plans. By employing knowledge of the nursing process and the teaching/learning process, nurses can modify patient education in such a way that both the nurse and the patient will grow in a cooperative relationship.

The nursing process is an orderly sequence of steps, as is the teaching/learning process. There are many descriptions of the nursing process and the steps involved. For the purpose of this book, the following steps are used: assessment, diagnosis, planning, implementation, and evaluation. In this chapter, each of these steps is analyzed in conjunction with the teaching/learning process. The two processes fit very easily together and provide an excellent framework for developing a teaching plan and carrying it out.

Consider the five steps of the nursing process and how the teaching/learning process fits into each:

1. *Assessment*

   - The learner
     —ability to learn
     —readiness to learn
     —attitude and motivation
   - The teaching situation
   - The teacher

2. *Diagnosis*

   - Identify the problem
   - Establish nursing diagnosis statement

3. *Planning*

   - Establish plan of teaching (what, how, when, where).
   - Establish learning objectives.

4. *Implementation*

   - Carry out teaching.

5. *Evaluation*

   - Determine effectiveness of teaching.
   - Reteach if necessary.

It is evident that each of the steps of the process is used in the development of the teaching plan.

ASSESSMENT

Assessment of the Learner

Assessment of the patient and his significant others is paramount to the process of patient teaching. It is considered one of the most important steps, and without it patient teaching could be ineffective. Narrow[1] identified three criteria to be considered when assessing the patient:

1. Effective teaching depends upon an accurate and complete assessment.

2. Effective assessment is directly related to the nurse's communication skills.
3. Assessment is always the first step in any rational, deliberate activity.

Resources

Before beginning the assessment, consider the sources available to provide needed information concerning the patient's educational needs:

- patient
- family members
- patient's chart
- nursing care plan
- other health professionals
- standardized teaching plans for specific diagnosis
- literature regarding teaching context for specific diagnosis.

The patient is the best resource. Through interviewing the patient, many factors that can influence his learning can be identified: attitudes toward learning; motivation; interest and readiness to learn; and medical, social, cultural, and educational background. All of these are determinants in identifying the patient's educational needs and abilities.

Family members and significant others also can offer valuable information. They can give insight into the patient's past experiences and attitudes toward patient teaching. Many times, significant others can identify problems the patient may not have felt comfortable discussing with the nurse at the time of the interview. The family members should be assessed for their value as resource and support persons for the patient and be considered potential learners of whatever is being taught.

Both the patient and family members can offer information regarding values and beliefs, activities of daily living, routine coping mechanisms, stress or concerns, hobbies, psychoemotional adjustment to the diagnosis, likely areas of noncompliance, support systems, comprehension level, useful teaching techniques, and possible motivations. All of these are necessary in planning adequate teaching.

The patient's chart and nursing care plan are excellent sources of information. The medical diagnosis, prognosis, and current treatment regimen should be clearly spelled out. The patient's response to these items should also be present. Notes from other health care professionals can contribute valuable information. The nursing care plan should offer information about unique individual characteristics, goals of the present illness, daily life style modification, nursing interventions and response, and significant others' resources. One might question if it is the hospital record or the home health record—it could be either. If the patient is a new patient just being discharged, the home health nurse should make every effort to contact the discharge planner. Otherwise, he may be a patient who has been seen by the home health agency and now has new educational needs. In either case, the chart and the nursing care plan offer invaluable information.

Other health professionals should also be included in the assessment of patients with teaching needs. The other professionals may include the physician, dietician, respiratory therapist, physical therapist, occupational therapist, speech therapist, and social worker. Team conferences in which the patient's teaching plan is discussed can be helpful in attaining new patient information, coordinating teaching efforts, and reinforcing information already taught. These conferences can be held in the hospital before discharge or during the course of care at the home health agency.

Standardized teaching plans and literature dealing with specific diagnoses can be very beneficial to the teacher. They can be used as tools in formulating the teaching plan. The nurse must be knowledgeable in the area she is teaching or be aware of and have access to available resources dealing with the content. One could not expect a nurse to do a good job teaching about the complications of chemotherapy if she had no knowledge about the drugs being given.

The Interview

When interviewing the patient and significant others responsible for his care, the nurse may use structured or unstructured interviews, conversations with the patient and/or significant others, and a checklist. Choose a time that is convenient and appropriate for the patient. If the patient is in pain or is having a stressful day, it is not a good time for an interview.

Both the nurse and the patient should be in a comfortable position. The purpose of the interview and the reason for asking personal questions should be explained. Questions should be formulated that will elicit the greatest amount of information in the shortest time.[2] Throughout the interview, be aware of verbal and nonverbal cues. The interview is a valuable tool of assessment.

Educational Needs

Identifying the patient's teaching needs is the goal of an educational assessment. Atwood and Ellis[3] made the following distinctions concerning needs. They identified four types:

1. A real need is one that is based on a deficiency that actually exists.
2. An educational need is one that can be met by a learning experience.
3. A real educational need indicates there are specific skills, knowledge, and attitudes to be attained to assist in attaining a more desirable condition.
4. A felt need is recognized as important by the learner.

Patients will often identify what their needs are, but nurses must still be in tune to needs not perceived by the patient, or at least question suspect health practices. Educational needs will determine the specific content to be taught. Chatham and Knapp[4] listed ten areas to consider:

1. normal body functions
2. health problems and diagnosis
3. medication prescribed
4. diet
5. activity limitations
6. diagnostic tests
7. preventative and/or health promotion activities
8. community resources
9. financial resources
10. future plans for the use of the health care system.

In home health care, much teaching evolves from the prescribed treatment. When assessing the patient's educational needs regarding prescribed treatment, consider the following questions:

- Why is it done?
- Who does it?
- When is it done?

- How long does it take?
- What is the cost?
- What is the patient required to do?

All of these questions will elicit needed information.

As there are many different areas of health teaching, the patient can have many different educational needs, and often these needs must be sorted. Chatham and Knapp presented five questions that should be considered by the patient, family, and teacher to help assess educational needs:

1. What should the patient know about his or her health condition(s), testing, treatments, prognosis?
2. What skills should the patient be able to perform in order to implement prescribed and recommended therapeutic or rehabilitative interventions?
3. What attitudes should the patient possess in order to adopt and integrate health-related skills and practices into his or her daily life?
4. What long-term health practices should the patient incorporate into his or her lifestyle?
5. What resources does the patient need to accomplish all of the above?[5]

Obviously, there are many areas and questions to be considered in assessing the patient for educational needs. The educational needs of the patient are a vital part of the assessment of the learner, but the readiness of the learner to learn is equally important.

Readiness To Learn

As the teacher, the nurse may have identified several areas for patient teaching, developed a well-organized teaching plan, and even attempted to carry out the plan, yet no learning may have taken place. The reason: the patient probably is not ready to learn. Learner readiness is vital to the teaching/learning process.

Narrow[6] described readiness to learn as the state of being both willing and able to use patient teaching. There are two types of learner readiness:

(1) emotional readiness, which is described as motivation or willingness; and (2) experiental readiness, which includes the patient's background of experiences, skills and attitudes, and ability to learn.[7]

In assessing the patient's readiness to learn, it must be remembered that it is closely related to ability, and that one's health or lack of health greatly influences one's readiness to learn. The patient may first, and rightly so, be concerned with such issues as pain, disability, disruption of personal life, and/or impending death. Narrow[8] identified four factors that influence the readiness of the learner: (1) comfort, (2) energy, (3) motivation, and (4) capability.

The patient's comfort can be divided into two types: physical and psychological. Regard for the patient's physical comfort would include assessing for pain, nausea, dizziness, fatigue, itching, hunger, and need to urinate or defecate. If any of these discomforts is present, very little learning can take place, if any at all. Common pyschological discomforts are anxiety, fear, grief, and anger. Effective learning is jeopardized if the patient is experiencing any intense emotions. The lists of discomforts presented are certainly not complete. The nurse must recognize the effect that discomfort can have on the patient's learning.

The patient's level of energy goes hand in hand with the patient's physical condition. The stage of illness, stressors, and any situational or maturational crisis should be considered, as all have a profound effect on the patient's energy level. Consideration should also be given to whether the patient is a morning or evening person, or if it matters. To teach someone a new skill when he is ready for his afternoon nap would be a difficult task for anyone.

Motivation was mentioned briefly in Chapter 1, and as the text continues, one will see that it is a major determinant of patient learning. Motivation was a basic component in the three models discussed in Chapter 1: Maslow's hierarchy, the PRECEDE model, and the Health Belief model. Motivation, in relation to health teaching, is defined as an emotional arousal that occurs in response to a health matter; once aroused, the individual will engage in health seeking behavior.[9] It is the force that moves people to action.

There are two types of motivation: (1) intrinsic motivation, which stems from Maslow's hierarchy of needs such as values, attitudes, perceptions, and/or unmet needs; and (2) extrinsic motivation, which comes from outside forces such as change in life style, family pressure, and/or environmental factors. It has been demonstrated that compliance will not occur if a patient has knowledge but is not motivated.[10] Patients must recognize that there is a need for information, and they must be physically and mentally ready to receive it before they can be motivated to learn.[11]

Patients may be motivated by many things. Some of these include the need or desire to know and understand, get well, be able to return to work, avoid complications, please others, and manage their own care. This list could be expanded to include many more items. Motivation is as individual as each patient. Any motivation to learn is a valid one.

The patient's capability to learn is one factor that can be observed, tested, and measured. Factors that affect capability include heredity, age, maturation, previous learning, physical and mental health, and the environment. The patient's physical and intellectual ability are very. important factors that must be recognized. If a patient is to be taught a psychomotor skill, his strength, coordination, dexterity, and senses must be considered. A patient with Parkinson's disease, diabetes, or visual impairments might have a very difficult time administering insulin injections or inserting contact lenses. The patient's math, reading, and verbal skills must be assessed. The patient who has difficulty reading should not be taught with printed materials. The patient with poor math skills may have difficulty preparing a mixed dose of insulin.

Learner readiness is essential to successful patient teaching and is a vital component of the assessment of the patient. The nurse must be knowledgeable and adept at initiating, assessing, and re-evaluating learner readiness.

Assessment of the Teaching Situation

Providing an environment conducive to learning should be one of the goals of any patient educator. To provide that environment, one must first assess what is present. There are three areas to be considered, all of equal importance to the teaching/learning process.

The physical environment is very important to patient learning. The room chosen for patient teaching should have comfortable physical surroundings, be comfortable for the patient and the teacher, and have minimal distractions. One should not attempt to teach wound care in a room where grandma is visiting with the next door neighbor and the four kids are playing. In the home, the nurse must judiciously choose the environment for teaching.

The interpersonal environment is one that nurses are usually quite capable of fostering. A relationship should be developed in which trust, caring, and mutual respect are present. In communicating with the patient, the nurse must be able to recall components of active listening. Nurses cannot just teach, they must listen to their patient, make eye contact, and question the patient for clarification. Ask the patient what his opinions are. Try to avoid writing or reading while the patient is talking. When speaking to the patient, use terminology that can be understood. All of these suggestions will help foster a beneficial interpersonal environment.

The external environment includes the resources and support that are available to the educational process. Resources include the people that are available as specialists or consultants. Time is always a valued resource. Nurses must develop skills that will enable them to establish the teaching situation quickly. Money and materials usually go hand in hand. Are there monies available to purchase teaching materials? Once the materials are available, is there someone to keep them up to date and organized?

Support in the external environment includes administrative support, by which many of the above resources would be made available. Physician support is imperative to providing patient education. One may consider this unnecessary, as the nurse is quite capable of identifying a patient's educational needs and providing the necessary teaching. But in home health, to receive Medicare reimbursement for teaching, the service must be ordered by the physician. Collegial support allows patient education to be consistent. Nurses working together in an agency should attempt to develop a mutual philosophy regarding patient teaching. Familial support has already been discussed to a great extent. The role families play in the teaching/learning process is evident. Support from all of these areas allows both the patient and the teacher to achieve an effective learning experience.

Assessment of the Teacher

All too often this aspect of assessment is ignored. Teaching has been identified as a responsibility of the nurse. But should every nurse teach, and is every nurse capable of teaching? Nurses must carefully examine their own beliefs. They might question if patient teaching is part of the care of every patient and if it is a patient right.

There are four factors to be considered when assessing one's ability to teach: energy, attitudes, knowledge, and skill. The nurse in home health can quickly acknowledge how much energy and time is consumed in patient teaching. Her attitudes toward patient teaching, the patient, and the subject matter must be considered. The more extensive the nurse's knowledge base, the more likely teaching will take place; as nurses practice, their knowledge base will grow. The last area to consider, that of skill, includes skills basic to teaching and skills related to a particular condition. Any nurse who is placed in the position of teacher should consider these four factors in assessing her abilities to teach the patient.

It is evident that assessment of the learner and family, the learning situation, and the teacher is paramount to developing a teaching plan. In assessing these areas, various assessment tools may be used and are often very helpful. Such an assessment tool is provided in Appendix C. Once the assessment has been completed, the process continues to the next step of establishing the diagnosis.

DIAGNOSIS

Once the nurse has completed the assessment of the patient, using all sources available, the problem can be identified and the nursing diagnosis stated. "Problem identification" and "nursing diagnosis" are often used interchangeably in describing the nursing process. "Nursing diagnosis is a statement that describes the human response of an individual or group that the nurse can legally identify and for which the nurse can order definitive interventions to maintain the health state or to reduce, eliminate, or prevent alterations."[12] The nurse arrives at the diagnosis after examining the information attained during assessment.

Since 1973, when the first meeting of the North American Nursing Diagnosis Association was held, the use of nursing diagnoses has grown greatly in the practice of nursing. There are now seventy-two approved diagnostic categories (see Appendix B). A nursing diagnosis consists of three parts: the title, etiological and contributing factors, and defining characteristics. The title is a concise description of the state; the etiological

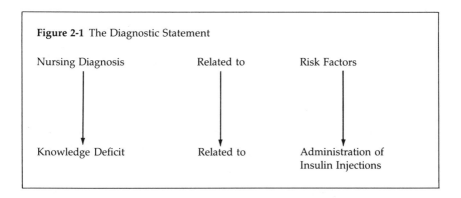

Figure 2-1 The Diagnostic Statement

Nursing Diagnosis	Related to	Risk Factors
↓	↓	↓
Knowledge Deficit	Related to	Administration of Insulin Injections

and contributing factors are physiological, maturational, or situational factors that can cause problems; and the defining characteristics are a group of signs and symptoms that are observed in the patient. The diagnostic statement has two components: (1) the diagnostic title, and (2) the etiological and contributing factors (Figure 2-1). The more specific the second part of the statement, the more specific the nursing intervention.

Some would think a nursing diagnosis would not be appropriate when developing a plan for teaching, but one of the 72 diagnostic categories is that of knowledge deficit.

Carpenito furnished a list of more than 200 medical diagnoses with associated collaborative problems and nursing diagnoses. She defined collaborative problems "as the physiological complications that have resulted or may result from pathophysiological and treatment related situations nurses monitor to detect their onset or status and collaborate with medical caregivers for definitive treatment."[13] Examples of collaborative problems would include paralysis, hypertension, malnutrition, and congestive heart failure, to mention a few. The diagnosis of knowledge deficit was associated with the majority of the collaborative problems listed in her book.

Her list emphasizes how important patient teaching is in nursing. The use of the nursing diagnosis "knowledge deficit" can become a part of every teaching plan. Through its use, the problem (knowledge deficit) and factors that contribute to the problem (e.g., dietary management of a low sodium diet) are identified. From the nursing diagnosis, the nurse can develop the teaching plan. The diagnostic category of knowledge deficit is described in Exhibit 2-1.

Exhibit 2-1 Knowledge Deficit

Definition	The state in which the individual experiences a deficiency in cognitive knowledge or psychomotor skills necessary for management of a health problem
Defining Characteristics	
Major (must be present)	Verbalizes a deficiency in knowledge or skill/requests information; expresses "inaccurate" perception of health status; does not correctly perform a desired or prescribed health behavior
Minor (may be present)	Lack of integration of treatment plan into daily activities; exhibits or expresses psychological alteration (e.g., anxiety, depression) resulting from misinformation or lack of information
Etiological, Contributing, and Risk Factors	
Pathophysiological	Any existing or new medical condition, regardless of the severity of the illness
Treatment-Related	Lack of previous exposure; complex regimen
Situational (personal and environmental)	Lack of exposure to the experience; language differences; information misinterpretation; personal characteristics: lack of motivation, lack of education or readiness, ineffective coping patterns (e.g., anxiety, depression, nonproductive denial of situation, avoidance coping)
Maturational	Lack of education of age-related factors; examples include: children: sexuality and sexual development, safety hazards, substance abuse, nutrition; adolescents: same as for children, automobile safety practices, substance abuse (alcohol, other drugs, tobacco), health maintenance practices; adults: parenthood, sexual function, safety practices, health maintenance practices; elderly: effects of aging, sensory deficits

Source: Reprinted from *Handbook of Nursing Diagnosis*, 2nd ed., by L.J. Carpenito, pp. 65–67, with permission of J.B. Lippincott Company, © 1987.

PLANNING

With data collected and a diagnosis made, the nurse prepares her plan for teaching the patient. What, how, where, and when must be considered. Just as input from the patient and family was important during the assessment, so is their input during the planning phase. In developing the plan for the teaching/learning process, there should be some description of what the learner should be able to do after instruction. It is also helpful to include how well and under what conditions he should be able to do it. This part of the plan is called the development of learning objectives or goals. In the nursing literature, the terms "objectives" and "goals" are often used interchangeably. Some descriptions of the nursing process differentiate between them, but both terms refer to the anticipated outcome of some planned action.

In planning teaching, the term "learning objective" is most often used and is used in this discussion. Learning objectives are written using patient input and, if well established, should provide a means of evaluating the effectiveness of the patient teaching. Learning objectives serve many functions. They

- identify activities regarding content and methods to be used
- inform the patient of what is expected
- provide a means of evaluation
- promote continuity of the teaching activities when more than one discipline is involved
- enable priorities to be set regarding information the patient must have
- provide a guide for patient teaching, which should ultimately save time.

Learning objectives should be written in behavioral terms. All of the following should be included when developing objectives:

- behaviors the patient is expected to accomplish as a result of the teaching
- objectives that are patient-centered, including what the patient will do
- a clear, concise statement that includes an action verb and the criterion for measurement.

Objectives are categorized into three domains: (1) cognitive, (2) affective, and (3) psychomotor. The cognitive domain includes the recall or recognition of presented information. It deals with the development of intellectual skills and abilities. The affective domain describes changes in feelings and attitudes and is related to the patient's values. The psycho-motor domain deals with the acquisition of motor skills. Usually, in patient teaching, the objectives are categorized in the cognitive and psychomotor domains, although this does not mean the affective domain is always excluded.

Objectives are also classified according to their order and complexity. Bloom[14] offered the following classifications for the cognitive domain, starting with the least complex:

- knowledge
- comprehension
- application
- analysis
- syntheses
- evaluation.

For the purpose of this book, the first three classifications are described more fully, as they will be the ones most likely used in patient education.

The following action verbs can be used in writing objectives concerning knowledge:

- count
- define
- identify
- list
- recall
- record
- report
- state.

The number of objectives written for each patient is as variable as each patient is individual. The nurse must use data from the assessment to establish objectives and to set priorities. There are certain learning objectives that must be included in the teaching plan. They are essential to the patient's safety and survival. They include learning needs that relate to basic physiologic and safety needs and usually include the areas of medications and treatments.

Once the learning objectives have been established, the nurse can further develop the teaching plan. The content to be taught and teaching strategies to be used should be considered. Obviously, content will depend on the patient's problems. (Chapters 7 through 13 deal with specific conditions and diagnoses that may be seen in the home setting.) The teaching strategies chosen will also depend on the individual patient, as not every method is beneficial to every patient.

There are many different teaching methods. The methods discussed below are ones we believe would be beneficial to nurses in home health.

Lecture	This is one of the most commonly used teaching methods. The teacher presents the needed information, often enhancing it with audiovisuals. When lecturing, the teacher should always allow for questions and/or discussion. Time limits should be placed on lectures, since the patient can become bored with the method.
Group Discussion	This method is most often used to present needed skills. It can also allow for return demonstration by the patient. The teacher must be sure the patient can see and hear what is being done.
Role Playing	This method goes hand in hand with demonstration. The teacher can present a situation and have the patient act it out. This allows for discussion of various situations that could arise.
Programmed Instruction	Prepared materials are used for this method. The patient can work at his own pace, but still must be self-motivated and literate. All programs should be closely evaluated before given to patients.
Contracts	Using this method, the nurse and the patient enter into an agreement, usually in writing. The contract usually specifies what is to be learned, how it will be learned, how long it will take to learn, how the learning will be evaluated, and, possibly, a reward. This method often increases the involvement and responsibility of the learner and can accommodate difficult styles of learning.
Media	Media may include pamphlets, films, printed materials, models, audiotapes, and videotapes. When using media, the nurse must recognize that the patient usually must be able to see, hear, and read. All audiovisual material should be reviewed carefully before choosing it for patient use. The nurse should determine that it is essential to needed teaching and doesn't just add fluff.

As the plan develops, the nurse chooses teaching methods and/or media. They should always coincide with stated objectives. In planning, the nurse must always depend on patient input and develop each plan with the patient's individuality in mind.

IMPLEMENTATION

The nurse should begin to carry out the intervention just as any other nursing intervention. The nurse should be prepared and knowledgeable in the content presented, always keeping in mind the assessment of the learner and his abilities. The teaching should be paced to meet the needs of the patient. Just by taking responsibility for the teaching role, the ability to teach and self-confidence will increase. These guidelines should prove helpful in implementing the teaching plan:

- Repeat information often.
- Try to allow the patient to use the information learned without delay.
- Reinforce all information presented.
- Praise the patient frequently and inform him of progress.
- Express enthusiasm and concern through voice and body language.
- Let the patient share what he knows about the subject.
- Take your time; don't rush the patient.
- Be flexible; adjust learning goals as necessary.
- Reward if beneficial.
- Provide a conducive learning environment.
- Communicate the importance of learning.
- Communicate your enjoyment in teaching the material.

These are only guidelines, and as the nurse develops skills as a teacher, many of these will become second nature. One must work at becoming a good teacher. The act of teaching becomes an art only through the continual incorporation of the process into daily practice.

EVALUATION

This step is the most neglected component of the process. The nurse can know the worth of the teaching only through evaluation.

When evaluating the teaching/learning process, two areas should be examined: (1) teaching effectiveness, and (2) teacher performance. The effectiveness of the teaching is measured by the behavioral objectives and what the patient learned. This can be done through return demonstration, written tests, analysis of laboratory data, compliance with the plan, and/or a follow-up questionnaire. The performance of the teacher can be evaluated through written or direct feedback from the patient.[15] The nurse may also consider videotaping a session or having a colleague present to evaluate a session. Evaluation is often intimidating to many nurses but is necessary for continued self-growth. Evaluation should be based on mutual trust and respect.

If it was determined that the teaching was unsuccessful or incomplete, the process begins again: assessment, diagnosis, planning, intervention, re-evaluation. The nurse can never assume that the patient learned or that teaching was effective. The teaching/learning process is never complete until evaluation occurs.

As the nurse becomes involved in the teaching of patients and the use of the nursing process, she becomes aware of the individuality of each patient. His values, motivations, life experiences, and response to learning are encompassed in this individuality. Through using the nursing process, the nurse can recognize the patient as an individual and provide and deliver a teaching plan that was formulated specifically for him.

NOTES

1. B.W. Narrow, *Patient Teaching in Nursing Practice* (New York: John Wiley & Sons, 1979).

2. Ibid.

3. H. Atwood and J. Ellis, "Concept of Need: An Analysis for Adult Education," *Adult Leadership* 19 (1971):210–212.

4. M. Chatham and L. Knapp, *Patient Education Handbook* (Bowie, Md.: Robert J. Brady Co., 1982).

5. Ibid.

6. Narrow, *Patient Teaching in Nursing Practice.*

7. B.K. Redman, *The Process of Patient Education,* 5th ed. (St. Louis: C.V. Mosby Co., 1984).

8. Narrow, *Patient Teaching in Nursing Practice.*

9. K. Dracup and A. Meleis, "Compliance: An Interactionist's Approach," *Nursing Research* 31, no. 1 (January/February 1982):31–36.

10. S. Cohen, *Education: New Directions in Patient Compliance* (Lexington, Mass.: Lexington Books, 1979).

11. D. Falvo, *Effective Patient Education* (Rockville, Md.: Aspen Publishers, Inc., 1985).

12. L. Carpenito, *Handbook of Nursing Diagnosis,* 2nd ed. (Philadelphia: J.B. Lippincott Co., 1987), p. x.

13. Ibid., p. ix.

14. B.S. Bloom, *Education Taxonomy of Educational Objectives: The Classification of Educational Goals, Handbook I: Cognitive Domain* (New York: David McKay Co., Inc., 1956).

15. M. Stanton, "Teaching Patients: Some Basic Lessons for Nurse Educators," *Nursing Management* 16, no. 8 (October 1985):59–62.

BIBLIOGRAPHY

Auerback, M. "Changes in Home Health Care Delivery." *Nursing Outlook* 33, no. 6 (November/December 1985):290–291.

Carpenito, L. *Nursing Diagnosis: Application to Clinical Practice.* Philadelphia: J.B. Lippincott Co., 1983.

Cross, K. *Adults as Learners.* San Francisco: Jossey-Bass Publishers, Inc., 1981.

Duffy, K., and Rankin, S. *Patient Education: Issues, Principles, and Guidelines.* Philadelphia: J.B. Lippincott Co., 1983.

Eagleton, B. "Contract Learning: An Effective Teaching Learning Strategy." *Focus on Critical Care* 11, no. 6 (December 1984):18–23.

Green, L. *Health Education Planning: A Diagnostic Approach.* Palo Alto, Calif.: Mayfield Publishing Co., 1980.

Knowles, M. *The Adult Learner: A Neglected Species,* 2nd ed. Houston: Gulf Publishing Co., 1978.

Megenity, J.S., and Megenity, J. *Patient Teaching: Theories, Techniques and Strategies.* Bowie, Md.: Robert J. Brady Co., 1982.

Stanton, M. "Patient and Health Education: Lessons from the Marketplace." *Nursing Management* 16, no. 4 (April 1985):26–30.

Stanton, M. "Teaching Patients: Some Basic Lessons for Nurse Educators." *Nursing Management* 16, no. 8 (October 1985):59–62.

Chapter 3

Barriers, Problems, and Mistakes of Patient Teaching

Objectives

- To discuss common barriers to patient teaching, including lack of administrative support, poor resources, lack of time, conflict with other disciplines, and inadequate teaching skills.
- To explore problems that arise in teaching situations, including different age groups, terminally ill, and noncompliant patients.
- To identify mistakes commonly made when teaching patients, including assessment, negotiating goals, duplication, patient overload, poor timing, poor use of media, assumptions, and poor documentation.

3

As nurses become involved in patient teaching, they will find that the best laid plans can certainly go astray. There are some common barriers, problems, and mistakes that often arise in the process of patient teaching.

BARRIERS

Barriers to patient teaching can include lack of administrative support, poor resources, lack of time, conflict with other disciplines, and inadequate teaching skills.[1] This list is not inclusive of all barriers, but consists of the most commonly encountered ones.

Lack of administrative support can lead to problems with all the other barriers listed. If the administration does not believe in the same goals of patient teaching as the nursing staff does, conflict is imminent. The biggest problem that arises is a lack of finances, which leads to not enough staff and an inadequate amount of audiovisual material and/or equipment. Nurses, as educators, must educate administrators concerning the importance of patient teaching and show them that the benefits of patient education are worth its cost. In home health, administrators should be more aware of its importance since it is one of the three reimbursable skilled services identified by Medicare in HIM-11, Section 204.4. Certainly, the identification of the need for patient teaching and adequate documentation by the nurse are recognized as important.

Resources to be considered might include human, monetary, and audiovisual. Human resources are the people available to teach. Home health agencies need nurses who are able to teach or who are at least willing to learn and take it on as a major responsibility. Having adequate numbers of nurses to perform patient teaching is necessary. If a nurse has more than six visits to make in one day, there will probably be little time for teaching.

Audiovisual material and equipment can be very important to patient teaching, yet there is effective patient teaching that takes place daily without fancy audiovisual materials and equipment. All materials and equipment should be carefully evaluated, considering the current and future needs of the agency. If affiliated with a hospital with a patient education department, the agency can possibly share such resources. Nurses involved in patient teaching should become aware of resources that have teaching materials available (see Appendix E).

Lack of time can be due to factors such as not enough staff, high patient load, and poor organization. An agency must look carefully at the patient population needing education and make schedules that allow for such activities. The nurse must also look at her personal organizational skills and decide how teaching plans can fit into her daily schedule. Some teaching can be accomplished in coordination with other skilled services being rendered.

Conflict with other disciplines can occur quite easily if there is no coordination of teaching activities. All too often, one discipline believes that it is the best qualified to teach a patient and does so without inquiring into what was taught previously by another discipline seeing the patient. This can lead to duplication of teaching, for which Medicare denies payment. Through coordination with all disciplines involved in the patient's care, such denials can be eliminated.

There are times when one discipline may be the best to teach a certain subject matter. The occupational therapist may be the most qualified to help the stroke victim feed himself again. The solution to overcoming this barrier is having one person coordinate the teaching needed. The nurse is usually the best choice, due to the assessment done and the amount of time spent with the patient. Team conferences can curb duplication of services. All members of the health care team involved in the care of the patient should be a part of the conference, including the patient and his family. It must be kept in mind that having the patient attend the conference is not always possible in home health Medicare-certified agencies due to home-bound requirements. If this is the case, the nurse must act as a strong patient advocate and represent her patient at the conference. Through collaborating and communicating with the other disciplines, this barrier is lessened.

The barrier of inadequate teaching skills was identified in both Chapters 1 and 2, but due to its impact on effective teaching, it is reiterated. Stanton stated: "wanting to help and knowing how to help are two different matters."[2] The nurse must evaluate her teaching skills and update and seek knowledge where needed. Those who hire nurses for home health should consider the nurse's background, her ability to teach, and her philosophy regarding patient teaching.

PROBLEMS

Besides barriers to patient teaching, there are problems with which patient educators must deal. These include dealing with different age groups, the terminally ill, and noncompliant patients.

In Chapter 1, characteristics of adult learners were discussed, and it is evident that adults do learn differently. In home health, the nurse may also deal with children, but the teaching will most likely be directed to adults.

In teaching children, one should schedule short sessions and make the teaching plan flexible and creative. Parents should be included in the teaching of small children. The child's developmental stage and cognitive level must always be considered. Incorporating play into the plan is a most effective teaching strategy. In teaching adolescents, the nurse can present much of the same material used with adults. Assumption of knowledge of anatomy and physiology is often a problem. An adolescent may allude that he is knowledgeable when, in fact, his knowledge is minimal. It is usually best not to include parents with adolescents. Remember to be very honest.

The characteristics of the adult learner obviously apply to the elderly, yet there are special considerations. Elderly patients are often more difficult to teach to alter behaviors. Try to keep changes to a minimum, provide a constant environment, and make few schedule changes. Information should be presented at a slower rate to allow more time for synthesis. Make sure the patient's vision is adequate to read any printed material you offer. Watch the patient closely during teaching sessions for decreased capacity due to cerebral changes. All of these suggestions will help in teaching the elderly.

Patient teaching for the terminally ill patient is a controversial issue. The terminally ill patient is one patient whom some feel does not need patient teaching. This certainly is a matter of opinion and depends on one's personal philosophy of patient teaching. Teaching the terminally ill offers hope and allows choices. In providing the patient with choices, he may be able to feel some sense of control over his environment. Medicare may not pay for teaching the terminally ill. This is explained further in Chapter 5.

In Chapter 2, the need for patient compliance was discussed, but little was said concerning noncompliance. Noncompliance occurs much more than the health professional realizes. Cohen[3] estimated that only one third of chronically ill clients adhere to their therapeutic regimens; one third are noncompliant because they adhere to a misunderstood regimen; and one third are knowingly noncompliant. In teaching patients about their therapeutic regimen, they may recognize it as an effective regimen, but unless they comply, this is not sufficient.

It is believed that nurses can do some things that might influence patient compliance:

- Establish a close, caring relationship.
- Assess the patient's beliefs and values concerning his health.
- Allow the patient to question what is being done.
- Reinforce the benefits of the prescribed regimen.
- Praise the patient frequently.
- Offer realistic expectations to the patient.

Although being cared for in the home has many advantages, the nurse must be aware that it is a place where it is very easy to be noncompliant. Once home, a patient often forgets the regimen carried out in the hospital and returns to old habits. Consider the following when dealing with patient teaching in the home:

- Compliance is the destination.
- Knowledge is the vehicle to reach the destination.
- Motivation is the energy that runs the vehicle.

MISTAKES

When doing patient teaching, mistakes are made. But it is through these mistakes that one can learn. The following is a list of mistakes and a brief discussion of each:

Assessment	This step has already been identified as one of the most important components of the teaching/learning process. Poor and ineffective assessments lead to a poor and inadequate teaching plan. Always confirm information obtained. Many times, illiterate patients end up with printed teaching material. Always reassess.
Failure To Negotiate Goals	One often forgets that the goals established are (or should have been) the patient's goals. The nurse may have goals, but patient goals should be given priority. Recognize when the goals need to be renegotiated. Unrealistic goals lead to noncompliance.
Territoriality and Duplication	Nurses can become very possessive of their patients and may want to be the only person available to them. They also feel personally responsible for the patient's teaching. One must remember that the patient is ultimately responsible for his behavior. Duplication of information often happens when the patient goes from the hospital to home and if the home health nurse changes. This can be solved with patient care conferences and good documentation of patient teaching.
Patient Overload	Too often, too much material is presented at one time. Shorter sessions are usually helpful in preventing this, and they allow the patient to synthesize and formulate questions. Be alert to the patient yawning, fidgeting, or being unable to answer questions. These may indicate overload and the need for a break in teaching.
Poor Timing of Patient Teaching	The nurse must consider the patient's schedule, physical comfort, and stress level. Very little learning can take place if the patient is in pain or anxious about something.
Poor Use of Media	Never use materials that have not been reviewed. This can lead to ineffective teaching and even very embarrassing moments. Know your material. Also, never rely solely on media for teaching.
Recognition of Patient's Background	There are times when the nurse seems to have forgotten the information gained from the assessment. Asking a patient who has financial problems to follow an expensive dietary regimen is unreasonable. The patient's ethnic, educational, and financial background is sometimes not remembered. The nurse too often teaches from previous background.[4]

Making Assumptions	Making assumptions is very easy to do but can be detrimental to effective teaching. The following *nevers* should be remembered:
	• Never assume that a patient understands the disease or prescribed treatment even if it has been diagnosed for some time.
	• Never assume that a patient knows why a prescription drug is taken.
	• Never assume because a patient is from a different socioeconomic, ethnic, or educational background that he will not be motivated or able to learn.
	• Never assume that because a patient has been noncompliant in the past that he will continue to be.
	• Never make assumptions!
Poor Documentation	This is surely a very common mistake and a very important aspect of patient teaching, especially in home health. Due to the critical impact documentation has in the Medicare home health program, Part II of this text covers documentation extensively.

All of the barriers, problems, and mistakes discussed here may have been encountered by some and probably will be again. Patient educators can learn from these mistakes and grow in their skills of patient teaching. Through knowledge of the teaching/learning process and enactment of the nursing process, nurses can assist their patient to meet the goals established in patient teaching and assist him in attaining an optimal level of health and well-being.

NOTES

1. M. Chatham and L. Knapp, *Patient Education Handbook* (Bowie, Md.: Robert J. Brady Co., 1982).

2. M. Stanton, "Teaching Patients: Some Basic Lessons for Nurse Educators," *Nursing Management* 16, no. 8 (October 1985):59.

3. S. Cohen, *Education: New Directions in Patient Compliance* (Lexington, Mass.: Lexington Books, 1979).

4. S. Rankin and K. Duffy, "15 Problems in Patient Education and Their Solutions," *Nursing*, April 1984, pp. 67–81.

BIBLIOGRAPHY

Becker, M.H. *The Health Belief Model and Personal Health Behavior. Health Education Monographs* 2 (1974): pp. 326–473.

Bennett, H. "Why Patients Don't Follow Instructions." *RN*, March 1986, pp. 45–47.

Carpenito, L. *Nursing Diagnosis: Application to Clinical Practice.* Philadelphia: J.B. Lippincott Co., 1983.

Dracup, K., and Meleis, A. "Compliance: An Interactionist's Approach." *Nursing Research* 31, no. 1 (January/February 1982): 31–36.

Duffy, K., and Rankin, S. *Patient Education: Issues, Principles, and Guidelines.* Philadelphia: J.B. Lippincott Co., 1983.

Eagleton, B. "Contract Learning: An Effective Teaching Learning Strategy." *Focus on Critical Care* 11, no. 6 (December 1984):18–23.

Falvo, D. *Effective Patient Education.* Rockville, Md.: Aspen Publishers, Inc., 1985.

Magill, K., Williams, S., Caspi, A. "Patient Education: Progress and Problems." *Nursing Management* 17, no. 2 (February 1986):44–49.

Megenity, J.S., and Megenity, J. *Patient Teaching: Theories, Techniques, and Strategies.* Bowie, Md.: Robert J. Brady Co., 1982.

Narrow, B.W. *Patient Teaching in Nursing Practice.* New York: John Wiley & Sons, 1979.

Redman, B.K. *The Process of Patient Education,* 5th ed. St. Louis: C.V. Mosby Co., 1984.

Ward, D. "Why Patient Teaching Fails." *RN,* January 1986, pp. 45–47.

Part II

Documentation of Patient Teaching

In Part I, information was provided to assist the nurse in assessing the teaching/learning process and in developing, implementing, and evaluating an effective teaching plan. Part II addresses the documentation of the teaching provided and the negative impact inaccurate and insufficient documentation can have on reimbursement of services rendered. Many nurses find documentation to be a tedious and unrewarding task that takes time away from patient care. Documentation is a necessary and important aspect of nursing care, including the area of patient teaching.

Three major roles documentation plays include the following:

1. to provide a record of the patient's progress and a means of providing a continuum of quality care
2. to alleviate a potential legal action or prevent a negative judgment in a lawsuit
3. to ensure reimbursement for services provided through third party payors (e.g., Medicare, private insurance companies, Title XX, workmen's compensation).

The emphasis in the following three chapters is placed on documentation to enhance reimbursement and prevent denials. This in no way negates the importance of the other two roles mentioned. We believe that if documentation is in-depth, descriptive, pertinent, and accurate, it should meet the needs of all three roles identified.

Chapter 4

Medicare Guidelines Regarding Patient Teaching

Objectives

- To define intermittent skilled care and homebound status according to Medicare guidelines.
- To identify factors utilized by Medicare to determine if a teaching visit can be considered skilled.
- To examine the reasonable and necessary aspect of patient teaching according to Medicare.

4

INTRODUCTION

Home health care became eligible for Medicare reimbursement with the creation of Medicare in 1965. The Medicare program provides reimbursement for care rendered by licensed nurses, physical therapists, speech pathologists, occupational therapists, medical social workers, and home health aides only under very specific and often times very limited circumstances. Not every Medicare beneficiary meets the criteria necessary to qualify for home health services coverage. Although it is recognized that services of an unskilled nature may be beneficial and of great importance to patients in their attempts to maintain, as much as possible, a normal existence at home, unskilled types of services are not covered under existing Medicare program regulations except as an extension of a skilled service, e.g., occupational therapy and home health aides.

It should be emphasized that Medicare does not provide coverage for general health care guidance, maintenance services, preventative illness training, and in general, the meeting of socioeconomic or emotional needs of patients. These aspects of patient care are essential to the patient's well-being and are integral components in providing quality care. But they do not constitute skilled services under the Medicare program and are not reimbursable unless provided in conjunction with a covered skilled service.

Skilled care has three components that distinguish it from unskilled care, which does not require professional health training. One compo-

51

nent is the observation and/or assessment of the patient. The patient's condition is such that the reasonable probability exists that significant changes may occur that would require the skills of a professional to evaluate the need for modification of the plan of treatment. It is considered medically reasonable and necessary for a professional to supplement the physician's personal contact with the patient; however, only the physician may order needed changes in the plan of treatment.

Another component is the giving of direct skilled services to a patient when the ability to provide such services requires the knowledge, skills, and judgment of a professional.

A third component, the one we are concerned with in this text, is the teaching of the patient and/or caregiver to carry out the appropriate services and observations. In addition to the requirement of an intermittent skilled need, the beneficiary must also be under the care of a physician and confined to his or her home.

Intermittent Skilled Care

"Intermittent" is defined in Section 204.1 of HIM-11. In order for the patient to meet the intermittent requirement, he must have a medically predictable recurring need for skilled care at least once every 60 days. There are certain exceptions to the 60-day limitation:

- a *silicone* catheter change that is required only at 90-day intervals
- manual fecal disimpaction that is likely to recur but is impossible to predict
- skilled observation for changes in the level of care at 90-day intervals for a blind diabetic patient who self-injects insulin.

Another exception to the intermittent requirement is when a patient expires or is institutionalized after the first skilled visit and the home health agency had no way of knowing this would occur. In this instance, the one visit would be reimbursable; however, a one-time visit to give an injection, draw blood for laboratory studies, or make a skilled observation and report to the physician would not be considered intermittent because its recurrence is not medically predictable.

Daily visits are also an exception to the intermittent requirement and are coverable if justified in writing by the patient's attending physician indicating the medical necessity for the visits and expected period of time they will be needed. Daily visits as defined by the Health Care Financing Administration (HCFA) may be 5, 6, or 7 days per week, depending on the particular fiscal intermediary's definition.

It has been our experience with fiscal intermediaries in HCFA Region VI that "daily visits" was interpreted to mean 7 days per week. We have dealt with denials of reimbursement because the patient was not seen on Saturday and Sunday. The fiscal intermediary's rationale was: if the patient and/or caregiver did not need skilled intervention on the weekend, was it necessary to see them 5 days per week? This could have been avoided by specific documentation of the situation. For example, the daughter was an R.N. but lived 200 miles away and was home with her mother only on infrequent weekends.

Due to the increase in home care since the inception of the prospective payment system (PPS) and advances in medical technology for the delivery of high-tech care in the home, e.g., mechanical ventilation, infusion therapy, multiple visits in a 24-hour period have become necessary. These multiple visits are reimbursable if they are reasonable and necessary and are not for an extended period of time. If the patient's needs could be met more effectively and safely in an institutional setting, the visits would probably be denied. These types of cases are usually referred to Level III of the medical review process for a claim determination. This is discussed in Chapter 6.

In May 1984, HCFA issued a policy statement that clarified the definition of "intermittent," but it is an issue that is still not completely resolved. Home care standards of practice are changing more rapidly than the government programs that regulate the Medicare-certified home health agencies. As home health care providers, we must stay in tune with the changes and become active leaders in the local, state, and national organizations concerned with improving the standards of practice in home care; increasing the awareness of legislators, both local and federal, of issues that need to be assessed and resolved in home care; and educating the general public concerning services available in their home.

Homebound Status

As mentioned previously, the patient must be confined to his home, i.e., homebound, to qualify for home health benefits under the Medicare program. Homebound requirements are found in HIM-11, Section 208.4 and as a cross reference in more detail in *Medicare Intermediary Manual,*

Part 3: Claims Process (HCFA Publication no. 13-3). See Appendix D for information on ordering these manuals.

The following is an overview of the homebound criteria found in these references:

- physician certifies that the patient is confined to his home
- patient's medical condition restricts his ability to leave home without the aid of a supportive device, special transportation, or the assistance of another person
- absence from home requires a considerable and taxing effort
- absences from home are infrequent and for a short period of time
- absences from home are to receive medical treatment
- absences from home do not indicate the patient is able to seek medical treatment outside the home.

Be aware that these criteria may be interpreted differently by your fiscal intermediary. It is the nurse's responsibility to understand the homebound criteria and apply them judiciously to each patient qualifying with functional limitations. The patient's diagnosis or condition may not be enough to qualify for the homebound criteria, e.g., diabetes mellitus, cardiac condition, cancer.

WHAT CONSTITUTES A SKILLED TEACHING VISIT

Under the Medicare program, the home health benefit reimburses only for intermittent skilled services required during the acute and subacute phases of an illness or injury. Once the patient's condition stabilizes, services are no longer reimbursable.

Skilled teaching of a responsible adult to irrigate a catheter, prepare and follow a therapeutic diet, carry out therapeutic exercises, administer injections, if appropriate, and be aware of signs and symptoms that should be reported to the physician can be initiated during the acute or subacute phase of illness. The patient's care may be continued when the skilled services of observation and evaluation or direct skilled care are no longer required. Therefore, to teach the patient self-care (and/or instruct the caregiver in the care of the patient) is one of the most important skilled services provided as a home care benefit, as it greatly contributes to the goals of recovery and rehabilitation.

There are several factors used by Medicare to determine if a teaching visit constitutes a skilled service, the foremost being whether or not the teaching provided requires the skills and knowledge of a professional (or if the teaching could be provided by the average nonmedical person). For example, the patient who has edema in his lower extremities and is instructed by the nurse to elevate his feet would not qualify because the average nonmedical person possesses enough knowledge to instruct the patient to elevate his feet.

Even though a skilled procedure is taught to the patient or caregiver, the procedure or service can still be performed by the home health care professional as a skilled service.[1] For example, for instruction in self-irrigation of a colostomy, both the teaching and performance of the service are considered skilled; therefore, when the patient has mastered the procedure, he is functioning as a skilled person. However, if the patient is unable to or physically or mentally incapable of learning the procedure being taught, and there is no one else available or willing to be taught, the performance of the procedure will continue to be considered a skilled service if performed by the nurse.[2]

On the other hand, a service is not considered a skilled service simply because it is performed by or under the direct supervision of a licensed nurse or therapist. When the nature of a service is such that it can safely and adequately be self-administered or performed by the average non-medical person without the direct supervision of a licensed nurse or therapist, it is an unskilled service without regard to who performs it. However, if the nurse provides personal care to a bedridden patient while teaching the caregiver how to care for him, this service would be considered skilled during the teaching phase because the knowledge of a professional is required to instruct in the care of a bedridden patient. On the other hand, even if no one was available or willing to learn to provide personal care, it would not constitute a skilled service even though it was performed by a nurse.[3]

TEACHING AND TRAINING ACTIVITIES THAT MEDICARE CONSIDERS REIMBURSABLE

HIM-11 lists twelve examples of teaching and training activities that are considered to require the skills or knowledge of a nurse or therapist, thus constituting a skilled service.[4] These twelve examples are incorporated in the following list:

1. Give an injection, e.g., insulin, B_{12}, certain antibiotics.
2. Irrigate a catheter, e.g., Foley, suprapubic, subclavian, Hickman.
3. Care for a colostomy, ileostomy, or gastrostomy.
4. Administer medical gases.
5. Prepare and follow a therapeutic diet.
6. Apply dressings to wounds involving prescription medications and aseptic techniques.
7. Carry out bladder training.
8. Carry out bowel training for incontinence *only*.
9. Perform self-care activities of daily living (dressing, eating, personal hygiene, etc.) through use of special techniques and adaptive devices when he has suffered a loss of function.
10. Align and position a bedbound patient.
11. Perform transfer activities, e.g., from bed to bed, bed to chair or wheelchair, wheelchair to bathtub or toilet.
12. Ambulate by means of crutches, walker, cane, etc.
13. Engage in therapeutic exercises when he has suffered a loss of function.
14. Care for a bedridden patient.
15. Care for an intravenous (IV) site.[5]

This is not an inclusive list; any teaching or training activity to be provided must be evaluated to determine if it constitutes a skilled service.

Through years of experience as Medicare-certified home health care providers, we have identified the following general criteria as tests that Medicare may use to determine coverage. The following questions can help you make this determination:

- Are the skills or knowledge of a professional nurse or therapist needed to accomplish the teaching?
- Are the teaching visits reasonable and necessary?
- Is the teaching pertinent to the active treatment of the patient's illness or disability?

Another important consideration involves the duplication of services by different disciplines seeing the same patient. For example, if a patient requires the skills of a nurse and therapist, each discipline must use its *unique* skill to instruct the patient in his care. This becomes crucial in the area of therapeutic exercises and activities of daily living. The patient may be receiving the services of a registered nurse, home health aide, physical therapist, and occupational therapist. It is of utmost importance that the patient's condition warrant the *unique* skills of the physical therapist and occupational therapist to carry out the physician's plan of treatment safely and effectively; otherwise Medicare may determine that these services could be carried out by the licensed nurse or, in some instances, performed safely and effectively by the home health aide. This determination could result in a denial of reimbursement for the physical therapy and occupational therapy services.

There are no hard and fast rules establishing a particular exercise program that would require the skills of a licensed nurse, physical therapist, or occupational therapist. Therefore, the responsibility falls upon the professional to document the patient's condition, indicating the degree of sensory perception, motor deficits, and loss of function. Proper documentation enables Medicare to make an accurate determination of the services covered.

As one of the major components of skilled care identified in the Medicare guidelines, teaching can be the only skilled service provided, but the need for teaching must be readily evident and requires in-depth documentation.

THE REASONABLE AND NECESSARY ASPECT OF PATIENT TEACHING

Teaching visits are subject to the test of reasonableness and necessity as outlined in HIM-11, Section 204.3. Reimbursement may be made for skilled nursing services required by an individual only if such services are found to be reasonable and necessary to the treatment of the individual's illness or injury. To be considered reasonable and necessary for the treatment of an illness or injury, the services furnished must be consistent with the nature and severity of the individual's illness or injury, his particular medical needs, and the accepted standards of medical practice.[6]

Among the factors Medicare uses to determine if a teaching visit is reasonable or necessary are

- the date of onset of the patient's illness or injury
- the length of stay in an institution, i.e., hospital, skilled nursing facility, or rehabilitation unit
- the length of service with the home health agency
- previous admissions to the home health agency for the same illness or injury
- physician's order for the teaching and training activities
- the consistency of the teaching and training activities with the nature and severity of the individual's illness or injury
- the learning ability of the patient's family member or caregiver being taught
- previous services from another home health agency
- mental status of the person to whom teaching is directed
- literacy level of the person to whom the teaching is directed
- patient compliance (indicate if noncompliance is due to a knowledge deficit or to patient will).

Teaching should never be initiated without first obtaining a physician's order. The order should be pertinent to and consistent with the patient's illness or injury. Teaching is an accepted nursing function and a vital part of good nursing practice, but in home health the physician must coordinate all care rendered, and therefore an order must be obtained.

Ensuring that the teaching and training activities are consistent with the patient's illness or injury is the first test in determining if the service is reasonable and necessary. This should be a part of your initial and ongoing evaluation process during the patient's entire length of service.

The date of onset is also very important to Medicare in making the determination of reasonableness and/or necessity. An example would be a patient who was diagnosed as a Type II diabetic 15 years ago, has been maintained by diet and oral hypoglycemics, recently experienced an acute exacerbation of the disease, and was placed on insulin injections daily. It would not be reasonable or necessary to continue home health visits after the patient mastered self-administration of the insulin injections just to instruct in an American Diabetic Association (ADA) diet of which the patient had a good understanding and to which he had adhered for 15 years. Consideration must also be given to whether the teaching provided in the home is reinforcement of teaching begun in the hospital, skilled nursing facility, or rehabilitation unit during a previous home health admission or is the initial instruction received by the patient for the particular illness or injury.

For reinforcement of previous teaching or training, fewer visits would generally be required and allowed than for initial training. For example, for a patient who had a cataract extraction and was seen by home health professionals postoperatively, visits to instruct him concerning signs and symptoms of complications to be aware of, dressings changes, etc. would not be covered for a second extraction since it would be expected that all teaching activities were completed during the previous admission for this illness. This would be true even if the patient was seen during the second admission by a different home health agency.

If the patient, family member, or caregiver being instructed has a learning deficit, poor comprehension, a condition that impedes memory, or is illiterate, the home health agency must document the need for additional visits. Although additional visits may be allowed in these circumstances, they cannot be allowed beyond the point where it would be appropriate to conclude that the individual cannot be taught to perform the required service.

For example, for a Type II diabetic patient who is placed on an 1,800-calorie ADA diet but shows poor comprehension and is a slow learner, additional visits might be allowed if these circumstances were included in the documentation of the patient's educational assessment, teaching plan, and visit record. Conversely, if the patient experienced intermittent memory loss or confusion and could not remember what had been taught during the previous visit, additional visits to instruct him would probably not be allowed since it would be doubtful he would benefit from additional instruction. In situations of this nature, a responsible family member or caregiver should receive the instruction.

Patient compliance must also be a consideration. The licensed nurse or therapist must assess and evaluate the reason for noncompliance. If noncompliance is due to will rather than lack of knowledge, it may be reasonably expected that the patient will not comply with the instructions, and the teaching and training activities should be discontinued if all avenues of teaching have been investigated and implemented and have failed. If teaching was the only reason this patient was on service, then visits should also be discontinued.

If has been our experience that length of service is very easy for Medicare to identify for any claim submitted. A claim submitted with teaching as the main skilled service provided with a length of service of more than 90 days will be reviewed carefully by the medical review department. We cannot emphasize enough the importance of documentation in these instances. If you have been instructing a patient for 60 days or longer, you must re-evaluate your teaching and his comprehension level and progress and determine in your professional judgment how much longer he will need the instructions of a licensed nurse or therapist. Your documentation should reflect this evaluation and your plans concerning the patient's specific need. Documentation is discussed in more detail in Chapter 5.

NOTES

1. U.S. Department of Health and Human Services, "Coverage of Home Health Services," in *Home Health Agency Manual*, Publication no. 11, Section 204.2C (Washington, D.C.: Health Care Financing Administration, 1983), p. 14.3.

2. Ibid.

3. Ibid., Section 204.2B, p. 14.3.

4. Ibid., Section 204.4B, p. 14.5.

5. Ibid.

6. Ibid., Section 204.3, p. 14.4.

BIBLIOGRAPHY

McHatton, M. "A Theory for Timely Teaching." *American Journal of Nursing* 85, no. 7 (July 1985):797–800.

Miller, A. "When Is the Time Ripe for Teaching?" *American Journal of Nursing* 85, no. 7 (July 1985):801–804.

Patient Teaching: Nurses' Reference Library. Springhouse, Penn.: Springhouse Corp., 1987.

Spiegel, A.D. *Home Healthcare.* Owings Mill, Md.: National Health Publishing, 1983.

Chapter 5

Documentation of Patient Teaching

Objectives

- To identify the rationale for documenting patient teaching.
- To identify potential problem areas in documenting patient teaching.
- To provide documentation guidelines.

5

INTRODUCTION

Documentation of the teaching plan provides the necessary information for the health care team to identify the teaching progress and new areas that need to be addressed, to assess and evaluate the effectiveness of the teaching plan, and to determine when a new or revised plan should be implemented.

Because the home health patient may be seen at various times by different disciplines representing the health care team, it is important that the teaching plan be reviewed and revised in the team conference meeting. This provides the nurse with a broader base of knowledge concerning the patient's learner readiness and ability. The team approach will help the nurse identify what time during the day the patient's mental acuity is at its peak and when the fewest interruptions can be expected, e.g., visitors, meal time, nap time, favorite television program. It is important that this information be documented on the assessment guide for future reference by the other team members. Discussing the teaching plan in the team conference meeting also makes the entire team aware of the teaching being done, enabling them to emphasize certain areas or encourage the patient during their visits.

The rationale for documenting teaching for the purpose of continuity of care and legal reasons is easily understood. But, in order to obtain reimbursement for teaching through the Medicare program and other third party payors, the development of an effective teaching plan and the thorough documentation of that plan are required. Refer to Chapter 4 for examples of teaching activities the Medicare program considers reimbursable and the general criteria Medicare may use to determine coverage of the teaching provided.

The "pitfall" of many home health nurses is documenting teaching in general terms. For example, if the patient lacks knowledge in the area of his medications, the nurse must remember that the medication being taught must be pertinent to the patient's condition or diagnosis, should be a newly prescribed medication, and the skills of a nurse must be required to instruct him in its actions and side effects and/or interactions with other drugs he may be taking.

To write "Patient instructed in action and side effects of Lasix" would be inadequate documentation. The following is a list of ten items that should be included in your documentation to enhance the chances for reimbursement:

1. date and time of teaching session
2. to whom the teaching is directed; if not the patient, why?
3. patient's and significant other's mental and health status
4. specific instructions given
5. teaching method used
6. patient's and/or significant other's level of comprehension
7. enhancements and/or barriers to the teaching process
8. goals that were met during the teaching session
9. evaluation of teaching session
10. plan for next teaching session.

Chapters 7 through 13 identify seven common medical diagnoses or conditions that may be seen in the home health care setting. Sample teaching plans and documentation guides for each are shown in these chapters. Remember: the teaching of a particular problem does not have to be accomplished in *one* session. Reimbursement can be obtained for several teaching visits if the reasonableness and necessity for the teaching are well-documented.

GUIDELINES FOR DOCUMENTATION TO ENHANCE REIMBURSEMENT

In Chapter 4 we discussed the Medicare criteria used to determine if a home health visit was skilled. The three components, observation/evaluation, hands-on direct skilled care, and patient teaching, were briefly defined. The tests of reasonableness and necessity, pertinence to the patient's condition, patient comprehension, and the requirement that the skills or knowledge of a professional are needed were also explored.

In this section, we identify some potential problem areas you may encounter in documenting your patient teaching. We provide examples of documentation errors, guidelines to assist you in improving your documentation skills, and the rationale to support the guidelines given.

Potential Problem 1:   Noncompliance
Documentation Error: "Patient experiencing elevated B/P of 196/100 to 188/90 each AM due to noncompliance of medication regime, i.e., Aldoril T.I.D."

Guidelines

1. Assess and identify why the patient is not taking his antihypertensive medication. Is it due to lack of knowledge or lack of will?
2. Document why the medication is not being taken:

   - If it is lack of knowledge, develop and implement a teaching plan.
   - If it is lack of will and there have been no changes made in the medication regime, and the patient has been identified as noncompliant and has reached a plateau, it is time to discharge the patient if no other skilled service is being provided upon conferring with his attending physician. Make the physician aware that the patient is noncompliant and that Medicare will not reimburse for maintenance or preventative care.

Rationale

- Identifying the knowledge deficit and establishing and implementing a teaching plan is considered a skilled service. To instruct in self-administration of oral medications is *not* considered a skilled service because it does not require the skills or knowledge of a nurse.
- Instructing the patient in the actions, side effects, and rationale for taking the medication requires the skills of a nurse and is reimbursable.
- If noncompliance is due to lack of will, continued teaching would not be considered reasonable or necessary and therefore not a covered service. The reason for denying continued teaching would be the

expectation that such teaching would not change the patient's condition.

Potential Problem 2:   Slow Learner
Documentation Error: "Reinstructed the patient in the seven exchange lists for a 1,800-calorie diabetic diet for 1 full day's caloric allocation. Sample menu left with patient."

Guidelines

This documentation would be questioned unless substantiated with additional documentation that would answer the following questions:

- What did the patient not understand?
- How many times had the exchange list been taught?
- Had a sample menu been presented before?
- How long had the patient been on an 1,800-calorie diet?
- How long has the patient been on service?
- How long has the patient been diabetic?
- Were the factors that caused the patient to be a slow learner identified in the initial assessment or have new factors occurred that affect the patient's learning ability?

Rationale

Reinstruction is not covered under the Medicare program unless documentation can substantiate its necessity. It is important in the home health setting that the teaching assessment, plan, and concurrent documentation is available to all nurses and health care team members since the patient may be seen by several nurses and this prevents the possibility of duplicated or repetitive teaching in the same area.

Potential Problem 3:   Confused Mental Status
Documentation Error: "Patient is confused at times. Instructed patient in diabetic foot care, e.g., cut toenails straight across, do not wear restrictive footwear, do not cut corns. Footcare instruction sheet left with patient."

Guidelines

If the patient is confused, the nurse needs to specify when and how he is confused. Is it intermittent confusion, long-term or short-term memory loss? Be specific as to the type of confusion associated with the patient. Is it drug induced and only temporary? The initial physical assessment and teaching assessment should reflect the same mental status and be considered in developing and implementing the teaching plan.

If the patient's confusion is such that it inhibits his learning ability, teaching should be directed to the significant other and so noted.

Rationale

Visits to teach a confused patient who does not have the potential for learning or retaining what is taught would not be considered reasonable or necessary. Therefore, the visit would not be reimbursable because the probability exists that the patient's condition will not be improved by the teaching provided.

Potential Problem 4:   Preventative Teaching and/or Instruction
Documentation Error: "Instructed patient in the seven warning signs of cancer. A written list of warning signs left with patient. Patient smokes two packs of cigarettes daily."

Guidelines

Preventative patient teaching is essential to the overall well-being of the patient. It is a patient's right as well as the nurse's responsibility to teach precautions, preventative interventions, and wellness. Provide preventative teaching in conjunction with a nursing service that is considered skilled by the Medicare program or private insurance company. Make certain the skilled service is well-documented and evident to the medical reviewer.

Rationale

In order for patient teaching to be a reimbursable service under the home health Medicare program, it must be pertinent to the condition or diagnosis for which the patient is being seen. Preventative or maintenance care or teaching is not considered a covered service.

Potential Problem 5:   Length of Service
Documentation Error: The patient has been on service for more than
                          60 days and the nurse is still teaching the patient
                          the signs and symptoms of his disease process,
                          therapeutic diet, and/or medications that have
                          not been changed since admission.

Guidelines

If the patient's condition and/or diagnosis has changed since admission, it should be clearly documented with the appropriate changes made in his care plan and teaching plan. A new condition with new teaching needs could increase the number of visits allowed.

If the patient has experienced an acute exacerbation of his admission illness, hospitalization, and/or change in the physician's plan of treatment, this would also allow an increase in the number of visits if properly documented.

Rationale

The test of reasonable and necessary would be used in determining coverage of teaching provided after 2 months of service. It is expected that teaching will be completed within 2 months of service unless exceptions are clearly documented.

Potential Problem 6:   Previous Instruction
Documentation Error: "Patient instructed in signs and symptoms of
                          infection in L eye post cataract surgery. Postop
                          1 day. R eye operated on 6 months ago."

Guidelines

Previous instruction accomplished while in the hospital or on service with another home health agency must also be considered. This is why it is so important to consult with the nurse or discharge planner who was responsible for the patient's previous teaching. This enables you to assess what has been taught and the patient's or significant other's level of comprehension. This should be a part of your initial teaching assessment.

Rationale

Visits to instruct in areas that have previously been taught are not covered due to the lack of reasonableness and necessity. It would be considered unnecessary to repeat previous instructions unless you can document a learning barrier that would necessitate reteaching.

Potential Problem 7: Providing Instruction When There is No Knowledge Deficit or When the Skills and/or Knowledge of a Nurse Are Not Required

Documentation Error: "Patient instructed to elevate his feet while sitting due to pitting pedal edema."

Guidelines

Teach only the areas for which the patient and/or significant other have an identified knowledge deficit and that the nontechnical medical person would not be expected to know.

Rationale

If the teaching performed is in an area in which the patient or significant other would be expected to have knowledge, it would not be reasonable or necessary for a nurse to teach. This would disqualify the teaching provided as a skilled service.

Potential Problem 8: Terminally Ill Patient

Documentation Error: "Instructed caregiver in aspects of the care of a bedridden patient, i.e., turning/positioning, bed bath, oral hygiene."

Guidelines

This documentation is not in error if the patient is currently bedbound. Teaching of the terminally ill patient is a controversial issue in fiscal intermediary medical review departments. Know your fiscal intermediary's philosophy.

The primary diagnosis should reflect the condition that requires skilled intervention. This may not be the terminal diagnosis, i.e., decubitus ulcer (L) heel, Stage III (primary diagnosis); CA of lung (terminal diagnosis). Teaching a patient's caregiver all aspects of terminal care, e.g., pain control, catheter care, administration of a complex medication regimen, would be covered if all coverage criteria were met. For example, the skill taught was complex and required the skills of a nurse to teach. The teaching is pertinent to the patient's *current* condition.

Newly diagnosed terminal patients may require several admissions. Once the patient reaches a plateau or becomes stable at a certain stage, he should be discharged. With a change in his condition, a new admission with different teaching needs would be warranted. The more complex the skill or activity being taught, the more visits required to accomplish your goal. Many simple skills would require one visit to complete the teaching. The nurse should schedule her visits accordingly. Any emotional support provided the patient or family should be given in conjunction with a skilled service. Documentation of the skilled service must be evident in the medical record.

Rationale

Teaching of the terminally ill patient must meet the same criteria as the teaching for an acute condition. To reiterate them: (1) requires a physician's order; (2) requires the skills of a professional; and (3) is pertinent to the patient's condition.

Even though the terminal patient and his family may need emotional support and coping measures to assist them in dealing with the situation, these are not considered covered services under the Medicare program.

Potential Problem 9:   Words and Phrases To Avoid
Documentation Error: "Reinstructed patient's wife in counting pulse rate."

The following words and phrases should be avoided:

- again instructed
- re-educated
- reviewed
- reinstructed
- encouraged
- urged
- reminded
- emphasized.

Guidelines

In our opinion, any word or phrase that indicates repetitive teaching should be avoided. The use of these words or phrases can be avoided by developing an individualized teaching plan specific to the patient's and/

or significant other's needs and abilities. If your teaching plan is evaluated and revised accordingly, the need to repeat previous instructions can be eliminated. The secret is to teach, in one session, only what the patient or significant other is able to comprehend. Remember: your teaching does not have to be accomplished in one session.

Rationale

The Medicare program does not reimburse for repeated teaching or instruction unless you can document the necessity for continued teaching in the area. As long as your documentation supports the tests of reasonableness, necessity, and pertinence to the patient's condition and requires the skills of a nurse, it should be reimbursed. If your visits are denied and your documentation supports all these tests, you have a basis to request that the case be reopened or to appeal the determination. Your documentation is your only means of justifying the skilled services provided!

The options available to you in overturning a denied claim are addressed in Chapter 6.

BIBLIOGRAPHY

U.S. Department of Health and Human Services. *Home Health Agency Manual,* Publication no. 11, Sections 255-268.5. Washington, D.C.: Health Care Financing Administration, 1983.

U.S. Department of Health and Human Services. *Medicare Intermediary Manual, Part 3: Claims Process,* Publication no. 13, Part 3. Washington, D.C.: Health Care Financing Administration.

Chapter 6

Medicare Denials: Prevention or Combat

Objectives

- To explore the Medicare medical review process.
- To explore the three Medicare medical review levels.
- To identify "helpful hints" to decrease potential denials.
- To explore the Medicare coverage compliance review process.
- To explore the post-payment review process.
- To explain the informal review of denied claims.
- To summarize the four levels of appeal processes available for Medicare Part A and B claims.
- To discuss the provision of waiver of liability for home health agencies under the Medicare program.

6

INTRODUCTION

In Chapter 4, we discussed Medicare regulations and criteria that must be met to ensure that the services provided to a Medicare beneficiary are covered under the Medicare insurance program. In Chapter 5, documentation was discussed with guidelines offered to assist you in documenting the services rendered. This book is dedicated to the skilled component of teaching because it has been identified as the most underdocumented if not the most underutilized skilled service covered under the Medicare program. Omdahl stated:

> Teaching is probably the most underdocumented skilled service because most nurses in home care do not recognize the scope and depth of teaching they do. The teaching is often done in an informal, conversational and sometimes reactive manner. Nurses tend to view much of their teaching as common sense suggestions. Yet, such suggestions are based on the nurse's professional education and experience.[1]

With this problem identified, it is easy to understand why a significant number of the visits denied reimbursement by your fiscal intermediary can be attributed to poor documentation.

All Medicare-certified home health agencies must deal with the denial of payment for services rendered. Denied services are frequently written off as free care by providers either because the patient has no means to pay or the provider is prohibited from billing the patient under the terms of the Medicare participating agreement it has with the Department of Health and Human Services to provide services to the Medicare beneficiary.[2]

Sources of revenue to absorb "free care" in a Medicare-certified home health agency are usually limited, necessitating an aggressive program to deal with denied visits. There are two approaches a home health agency can take: either the preventative or combative approach. In view of the time and expense necessary to obtain an overturned decision on a denied visit, prevention is by far the better option.

DENIAL OF REIMBURSEMENT

There are various means afforded a Medicare fiscal intermediary by HCFA to deny reimbursement for visits. They are medical review, coverage compliance review, and postpayment review.

Medical Review

In an attempt to standardize the intermediary home health medical review, HCFA established ten regional fiscal intermediaries (see Appendix D); mandated the use of HCFA forms 485, 486, 487, and 488; and established a home health medical review/utilization review work group composed of HCFA's central and regional office staff, the ten regional home health intermediaries, and the Blue Cross and Blue Shield Association. The purpose of the work group was to clarify medical review questions and issues. The ten regional intermediaries and required forms were created to standardize the payment or denial determinations in the medical review process.

All freestanding home health agencies began transferring to one of the ten designated regional fiscal intermediaries on October 1, 1986. Hospital-based home health agencies remained with the hospital's fiscal intermediary until January 1, 1988.[3] Before this, each state had to deal with one or more fiscal intermediaries including the Office of Direct Reimbursement (ODR). This created many inconsistencies among fiscal intermediaries and was more difficult and costly for HCFA to manage. The following are the mandated HCFA forms created in 1985:

- UB-82 (HCFA 1450): standardized billing form
- HCFA 485: Home Health Certification and Recertification Plan of Treatment
- HCFA 486: Medical Update and Patient Information
- HCFA 487: Plan of Treatment/Medical Update and Patient Information Addendum
- HCFA 488: Home Health Agency Intermediary Medical Information Request.

The medical review department of a fiscal intermediary is responsible for reviewing claims and medical records to determine if services billed by the home health agencies are in fact covered under the Medicare program and meet all criteria necessary for payment of the services. Other responsibilities include researching coverage issues and questions, performing coverage compliance reviews (onsite compliance audits) and postpayment audits or reviews, and investigating program integrity cases. Most fiscal intermediaries use three levels of review:

1. *Level I: Clerical review*

   - Review for completeness and accuracy of forms.
   - Microfilm claims and medical records.
   - Review to determine if services are in excess of specific indicators or parameters.
   - Determine to pay, deny, or refer to Level II.

2. *Level II: Registered nurse review*

   - Review for criteria of coverage.
   - Review for sufficient information to make a determination.
   - Request additional information in order to make a coverage determination.
   - Determine to pay, deny, or refer to Level III.

3. *Level III: Physician and/or specialty team review*
   - Review for standard of medical practice.
   - Review own specialty for coverage criteria, i.e., physical therapy, speech therapy, occupational therapy, and medical social work.
   - Level III does not make claim determinations for technical denials.
   - Determine to pay or deny.

Fiscal intermediaries may differ slightly in their review process. It is essential that you know your fiscal intermediary's organizational structure, the responsibilities of each designated department, and the process and/or persons responsible for reviewing your claims.

One of your management objectives should be to have as many claims paid at Level I as possible. This would decrease the length of time involved in making a claim determination, therefore increasing your cash flow if your agency is not on Periodic Interim Payment (PIP). The following "helpful hints" could be used to help meet this objective and possibly prevent denials at Levels II and III:

- Be familiar with the medical review team at your fiscal intermediary. Know what its philosophy and interpretations of the Medicare guidelines are.
- Educate your staff, both professional and support, concerning the proper completion of HCFA forms.
- Educate your professional staff in documenting the skilled services they render, homebound status, and medical necessity.
- Educate your nursing support staff (home health aides) in documenting the personal care they render and homebound status.
- Have a knowledgeable quality assurance person review patient progress notes for all disciplines; complete monthly chart audits of random records; and review initial evaluation, discharges, and all documentation submitted to the fiscal intermediary for claim processing.
- Develop an orientation program that includes Medicare coverage criteria, documentation guidelines, and completion of required HCFA forms.
- Reconcile the number of visits billed with the number noted in the medical record to ensure that accurate visit counts and documentation are available for each visit billed.

- Maintain a favorable waiver of liability status. When you are off waiver, you are automatically on 100 percent medical review. Waiver of liability status is discussed later in this chapter.
- Obtain less than a 5 percent denial rate on a coverage compliance review or postpayment review.

The options home health providers have in combating denials are addressed later in this chapter.

Coverage Compliance Review

Coverage compliance reviews are mandated in Section 2300 of the *Medicare Intermediary Manual* (HCFA Publication no. 13-3). See Appendix D for information on how to order this manual and other HCFA manuals or publications for reference. An overview of the coverage compliance review is given here. We suggest that you familiarize yourself with the Medicare regulations regarding the coverage compliance review in the *Medicare Intermediary Manual*.

The fiscal intermediaries are required by HCFA to conduct periodic onsite coverage compliance reviews annually for a specified number of home health agencies. The coverage compliance review is the same as an onsite compliance audit, which is the term most frequently used in the home health industry. The fiscal intermediary is required to give the home health agency a 24-hour notice by telephone, which is followed by a written notice. The fiscal intermediary is not required to inform you before their arrival for the audit of the records they will review. HCFA mandates that at least twenty beneficiaries' claims be reviewed, which accounts for at least 100 visits. These are to be selected from the beneficiaries who are currently or were recently on service. HCFA also mandates that the reviewer make home visits to at least five of the beneficiaries reviewed.

The minimum five beneficiaries selected for home visits will be based on beneficiaries meeting one or more of the following criteria:

(a) Beneficiaries who have been furnished services for six months or longer.

(b) Beneficiaries who require three or more different types of service.

(c) Beneficiaries whose records indicate a questionable need for continued home health services.

(d) Beneficiaries who have been furnished seven or more home visits per week.

(e) Beneficiaries who have been furnished less than four visits per month.[4]

Home health agencies are ranked according to the following criteria:

- the number of visits per patient
- the percentage of Medicare utilization
- the average Medicare cost per Medicare patient.[5]

Any agency that falls within the top 10 percent of the ranking is subject to selection by the fiscal intermediary for an onsite audit. Agencies that have been certified for less than 1 year and those with an unfavorable presumptive status are also subject to selection for an onsite compliance audit. These onsite audits are used by the fiscal intermediaries to determine if the home health agency is providing services according to the Medicare program requirements and if the medical records reflect the services that have been billed to Medicare.

Since the inception of HCFA 485-487, it has been easier for the medical reviewer to substantiate medical information submitted for claims processing with the patient's medical record, emphasizing again the importance of accurate and pertinent documentation. If your agency has a person who is responsible for completing the HCFA 486 for billing, it is essential that he or she has access to the current medical information for each medical record and schedules a case conference meeting with the professionals responsible for the case. One of the quality control measures should be to ensure that the medical record closely reflects the information written on HCFA 486.

The onsite reviewer has the authority to deny visits during the coverage compliance review. The regulations require the reviewer to make every attempt to resolve questions involving coverage and documentation before the exit conference of the coverage compliance review. Remember: the burden of proof rests with the provider, and every effort should be made to resolve these questions while the reviewer is still in your agency. Some fiscal intermediaries will allow you up to 2 weeks to submit additional information to support your claim and assist them in making a decision.

If the denial results from lack of documentation, for example, you billed eight skilled nursing visits one month and had only seven nursing visits documented, then one visit would be denied. There are no provisions that allow for late submission of documentation. This is why it is crucial that home health agencies' billing departments reconcile the number of visits billed with the number of visits rendered and documented. This is another preventative measure to use in decreasing denials during an onsite audit. Many home health agencies have neglected this check and balance system in their billing process, resulting in a large billing denial rate at onsite audit time. This is one area in which you have control and can prevent denials due to billing errors.

As mentioned previously, review Section 2300 of the *Medicare Intermediary Manual* for specific regulations relating to the coverage compliance review. Cabin cited the following minimum points that would be reviewed in each case:

(a) Is patient homebound? (Refer to Section 3120.4)
(b) Is patient's residence an 1861 (j) (1) facility? (Refer to Section 3120.5)
(c) Were services furnished under a plan of treatment? (Refer to Section 3120.3)
(d) Was the plan put into writing in a timely manner? (Refer to Section 3120.3, paragraphs 1 and 2)
(e) Is the plan complete? (Refer to Section 3120.3, paragraphs 1 and 2)
(f) Were changes or extension made in accord with policy? (Refer to Section 3120.3, paragraph 2)
(g) Did the HHA count the visits accurately? (Refer to Section 3124)
(h) Were length and frequency of aide visits accurate? (Refer to Section 3124.2)
(i) Were evaluation visits billed only when appropriate? (Refer to Section 3124.3)
(j) Were excluded services supplied? If yes, enumerate. (Refer to Sections 3125, 3150)

(k) Was the physician certification requirement met? (Refer to Sections 3128, 3326-3329)

(l) Were the services rendered medically necessary for treatment of the patient's condition? (Refer to Sections 3117, 3118, 3119)

(m) Were the visits appropriately classified by type? For example, were services billed as skilled nursing really skilled? (Refer to Sections 3116, 3119)

(n) Were medical appliances and/or medical supplies appropriately ordered and/or supplied? (Refer to Section 3119.3)

(o) Were the data consistent with the additional evidence to substantiate original payment? (Refer to Section 3600.1D)[6]

Most, if not all, fiscal intermediaries have always used some type of visit screening device, usually at Level I medical review, as one means to determine if the visit frequency exceeded the parameters and the claim should be referred to Level II medical review. With the mandated standardized billing form (UB-82), the physician plan of treatment form (HCFA 485), the medical information form (HCFA 486), and the ten regional fiscal intermediaries, it is easy for HCFA to develop national screens.

The home health prepayment screening module adopted by HCFA's Health Standards and Quality Bureau (HSQB) was the Wisconsin Screening Module developed by Wisconsin Blue Cross and Blue Shield. It is to be used by the ten regional intermediaries for home health claims processing and medical review, resulting in a more intensive medical review. HCFA requested that these not be provided to home health providers as they were only guidelines. HCFA did not want home care providers to use them as "absolutes." Each patient must be assessed and visits scheduled according to his particular needs. The prepayment screening module screens not only for number of visits per particular diagnosis or condition but for invalid or incorrect ICD-9-CM diagnosis codes for principal and secondary diagnoses, start of care (SOC) date for length of service, certification period for current physician's orders, invalid or incorrect Health Insurance Claim Number (HIC), and if the treatment week is counted as seven calendar days beginning with the start-of-care date.

As mentioned previously, third party payors usually follow Medicare's lead, and the prepayment screening module is no exception. All insurance companies are required to accept the UB-82 for billing, and some insurance companies have begun requiring that the physician's plan of treatment be submitted on HCFA 485.

The visit frequency must be established and ordered by the physician. It is the nurse's responsibility to inform the physician of her assessment of the patient and home situation. Most physicians would welcome a suggested visit frequency based on your judgment. The following are items to take into consideration when determining the initial visit frequency or subsequent changes:

- new diagnosis or condition
- acute exacerbation of a chronic or stable diagnosis or condition
- recent hospitalization
- recent medical intervention
- recent change in medical regimen
- complex skills requiring extensive teaching.

In most instances, visit frequency should begin aggressively and decrease as the patient's condition improves. Exceptions to this rule of thumb are conditions that go into remission, stabilize, or reach a plateau only to regress later. In such instances, the visit frequency must be adjusted accordingly. This is an area in which the home health nurse should become adept. If the denial rate exceeds 5 percent as a result of the onsite compliance audit, the home health agency is placed on 100 percent prepayment medical review for the next calendar quarter.

Claims or visits that are denied during the onsite compliance audit are entitled to the same appeal rights as the claims processed in the medical review department of the fiscal intermediary. The appeal process is discussed later in this chapter.

Postpayment Review

Postpayment reviews are covered in the *Medicare Intermediary Manual*, Section 3902.6. The fiscal intermediary may call this review a postpayment medical record validation or a postpayment medical record review. Medicare-certified home health agencies should familiarize themselves with Section 3902.6 and with the term used by their particular fiscal intermediary. It is vital that each home health agency know its rights and responsibilities during this review.

HCFA mandated these reviews after the creation of HCFA 485, 486, and 487. The record sampling is the same as in a coverage compliance review, with at least twenty beneficiaries' records being reviewed. Every home health agency is to have a postpayment review annually, which can be done in conjunction with a coverage compliance review. If the postpayment review is accomplished inhouse, any noncovered services identified will be calculated in the denial statistics for the quarter in which the postpayment review was done. If the postpayment review is conducted during a coverage compliance review, the noncovered services will be counted toward the coverage compliance denial rate.

The purpose of the postpayment review is to determine if the information contained in HCFA 485, 486, and 487 coincides with the information contained in the medical record. The following areas of the medical record are reviewed:

- accuracy of information submitted on HCFA 485, 486, and 487
- discrepancies noted with reason for occurrences
- appropriateness for previous payment decisions
- evaluation of form content.

The fiscal intermediary is to determine the appropriate corrective action to be instituted according to the number of medical records found to have inaccurate, erroneous, or insufficient information (see Table 6-1).

It is the fiscal intermediary's responsibility to notify the home health agency when a postpayment review is to be conducted. The agency usually has 2 weeks in which to submit the requested information if the postpayment review is to be an inhouse review. Each fiscal intermediary may have a different timeframe requirement. Know what it is. If the information is not received by the fiscal intermediary according to its timeframe, the claims can be denied on a technical basis for nonsubmission of documentation. The fiscal intermediary is to notify home health agencies of the results of the postpayment review within 6 weeks. The corrective action and timeframe in which to correct deficiencies are identified.

As mentioned earlier in this chapter, the fiscal intermediary has various options it can exercise to recoup payments of visits or claims submitted

Table 6-1 Potential Postpayment Review Results

No. of Records	Discrepancy	Corrective Action
*1–4**	Lack of pertinent information on HCFA 485/486/487	Provider education
*5 or more**	Medical record documentation does not support information on HCFA 485/486/487	100% medical review until problem is corrected
2 or more	Lack of documentation or inaccurate documentation resulted in denied services	Identify reason Provider education Intensified review Recoup inappropriate payment

*Discrepancies cited did not result in denied services.

previously and paid. Therefore, it is of utmost importance that the home health agency ensure that the information submitted to the fiscal intermediary on HCFA 485, 486, and 487 reflects the information contained in the medical record. It should be accurate, complete, and sufficient for the fiscal intermediary to make a claim determination in the initial medical review process.

Each Medicare-certified home health agency should have at least one person responsible for reviewing all forms and records before submission to the fiscal intermediary as well as maintaining a denial log for reference (see Exhibit 6-1). Attempts to prevent denials of noncovered services are easier and less time-consuming than combatting the denials once received, as will be determined by reading the rest of this chapter, which addresses the options providers have to combat denials.

REVIEW OF DENIED CLAIMS

The review of denied claims is an informal process and is not available to all providers because fiscal intermediaries are not required to offer such a service. The advantage of the service is that it is less costly and time-consuming than a formal appeal process. The following is a list of disad-

Exhibit 6-1 Denial Log

Patient Acct. #	Patient Name	HIC#	Reason for Denial	Paid WOL* Y N	Technical	Date Rec'd	Agency Decision Appeal Y	N	# of Visits Denied	Discipline	Period Covered	Date Appealed	Date/Status on Appeal	FYI Rationale
000715	Jane Doe	478-46-0501	Medical necessity	N	N/A	1/10/88	√		8	SN	9/1/87–9/30/87	1/20/88		Change in medical regime 2× in Sept.

*Waiver of liability.

vantages the home health agency should be aware of if this option is chosen to deal with denied claims:

- at discretion of fiscal intermediary whether or not to review a denied claim
- retroactive denials may result
- retroactive denials counted in waiver status of quarter denial issued
- low priority of fiscal intermediary
- no budget allowance to fiscal intermediary for review
- available only on claims not paid under waiver of liability
- jeopardize formal appeal if not resolved in appeal timeframe.

As evidenced, the disadvantages outweigh the advantages, but requesting a review is still a good option if the fiscal intermediary processes the review and makes a determination in a timely manner. Be aware of what term your fiscal intermediary uses to refer to the informal review of denied claims and the additional information submitted by the home health agency to substantiate the initial claim. Some fiscal intermediaries call it a "re-review," "review," or "reconsideration." "Reconsideration" is really an inappropriate term since an actual reconsideration is one of the formal appeal processes.

REOPENING OF DENIED CLAIMS

Reopening is outlined in Section 258 of HIM-11, the regulation governing the reopening process. Reopening is an option not only for the home health agency but for the fiscal intermediary. It is up to the fiscal intermediary to allow or disallow a request from the home health agency to reopen a denied claim. The home health agency must realize that the fiscal intermediary has the authority to make retroactive denials on reopened claims. The same advantages and disadvantages of a review apply to the reopening process.

Section 258 of HIM-11 identifies three reasons that the fiscal intermediary has the authority to reopen a Medicare Part A or Part B case, either paid or denied. They are summarized as follows:

1. for any reason if found to be incorrect within 1 year after the date of the original decision

2. for "good cause" within 4 years of the original decision (see Section 258 of HIM-11 for what is considered "good cause")
3. for reasons of fraud or similar fault, or if decision was made due to clerical error or an error on the basis of evidence available at the time of the original decision, there is no time limit on reopenings for these reasons.

The home health agency's request to reopen a claim coverage compliance review and/or a postpayment review could initiate reopening by the fiscal intermediary.

APPEAL PROCESSES: MEDICARE PART A AND PART B

There are four levels of appeal processes available for Medicare claims. These are summarized in Table 6-2 and Table 6-3 for Medicare Part A and Part B denied claims.

The Omnibus Budget Reconciliation Act of 1986 (OBRA: Public Law 99-509) changed the policy on a few items that affected the medical appeal process. It allowed the beneficiary to designate a representative to appeal his claim. This designated representative could be an employee of the home health agency responsible for his care. HCFA had issued a revision in 1984 (Transmittal 150) to HIM-11 prohibiting beneficiary representation by an employee of the home health agency. OBRA did state that the agency employee would not be reimbursed for any cost incurred while representing a beneficiary by either the Medicare program or the beneficiary. The law also made the Administrative Law Judge level available to Part B claims. Before this, Part B claims had only two levels of appeal available: (1) review by intermediary, and (2) hearing before a hearing officer designated by the intermediary.[7]

There are certain circumstances that must be met in order for Part B claims to be reviewed by the Administrative Law Judge. Cabin outlined these as follows:

• In a June 8, 1987, Supreme Court decision, it was found that "federal courts have jurisdiction under Part B to hear disputes over the 'method of reimbursement' as distinguished from the amount of benefits on an individual claim."[8]

- These two developments gave Medicare Part B denied claims the same appeal options as the Medicare Part A claims under certain circumstances.

- Technical denials were allowed the appeal right. The term "technical" is not addressed in the regulations but is used by HCFA and the intermediaries to differentiate between denials for medical necessity and reasonableness and denials for non-homebound status, lack of documentation, and lack of physician's orders.

Since there is no clear-cut definition of "technical," its meaning has been defined differently by the fiscal intermediaries. The home health agency should determine its particular fiscal intermediary's interpretation of its meaning and the manner in which it is used. Before OBRA, "technical" denials did not have an appeal right, so the visits denied for technical reasons were essentially lost as far as reimbursement was concerned.

The scope of this text allows only a brief discussion of the appeal processes available to the Medicare beneficiary and home health agency. Through knowledge of the coverage criteria and documentation techniques, denials can be prevented to a great extent. As you have realized in this chapter, prevention of denials is easier, less costly, and less time-consuming than the combative measures through the appeal processes.

WAIVER OF LIABILITY

A final rule published in the *Federal Register* on February 21, 1986, had eliminated the provision or the use of the favorable limitation of liability presumption for all providers, including home health agencies. However, the Consolidated Omnibus Budget Reconciliation Act of 1985 (COBRA) enacted on April 7, 1986, reinstated the favorable limitation of liability presumption for home health agencies who have a 2.5 percent or less denial rate until 1 year after the ten regional intermediaries begin servicing home health agencies.[9] The regional intermediaries began servicing home health agencies October 1, 1986. The transfer is anticipated to be completed October 1, 1987; therefore, it can be assumed that October 1, 1988, will be the implementation date for a case-by-case waiver of liability protection.[10] Medicare Part B claims have always been on a case-by-case basis, and this will not change.

Table 6-2 Medicare Part A Formal Appeal Processes

Appeal Option	Time Limit	Who May Appeal	Minimum Dollar Amt.	File with Whom
Reconsideration	60 days from receipt of denial notice*	Beneficiary Provider if beneficiary chooses not to request reconsideration and beneficiary's liability waived	None	SSA Admin. office HCFA, fiscal intermediary
ALJ	60 days from receipt of reconsideration decision	Same appellant as in reconsideration	$100 (excludes co-ins. and deduct.)	Reg. HCFA office SSA office Form HA 5011-U6 HCFA Form-2649
Appeals Council review	60 days from receipt of ALJ's decision	Same as began appeals process	$100 (excludes co-ins. and deduct.)	SSA office in writing
Federal District Court	60 days from receipt of Appeals Council decision	Same as began appeals process	$1,000 (may add visits to meet reqmt.)	Fed. Dist. Ct. in dist. of applicant's business or, if beneficiary, residence, or Dist. Ct. for D.C. File against Sec. of HH Svcs.

*Good cause exceptions are permitted for filing (Ref. 20 CFR 205.1813).

Who Makes Decision	Time Limit for Decision	Documentation Required	Notice	Next Level
FI	None	Original 485/486/487 Additional documents submitted	Appellant or rep.	Administrative Law Judge (ALJ) *Note:* HCFA and FI do not have input at this level.
ALJ appointed by SSA office	None	Record: • position paper • documentation to support claim and reversal denial *Note:* may be new evidence Personal appearance: • position paper • witnesses: —beneficiary's family, M.D., etc. —HCFA and FI • attorney, if desired	Appellant or rep.	Appeals Council review
Appeals Council appointed by HHS Sec. May accept or reject case for review If denied, ALJ decision final: go to next level (judicial review)	None	Documents from ALJ hearing New evidence Written brief Oral argument	Appellant (may request copy of evidence that supported decision)	Federal District Court
Court presumes Appeals Council's decision is correct. Burden of proof is on appellant to show that it is not. Decision is binding on appellant and government.	None	No new evidence permitted Written briefs Oral argument	Decision of court	Decision is binding on appellant and government with respect to facts and claims.

Table 6-3 Medicare Part B Appeals Process

Appeal Option	Time Limit	Who May Appeal	Minimum Dollar Amt.	File with Whom
Review	6 months from receipt of denial	Beneficiary or representative Provider if beneficiary chooses not to appeal	None	Insurance carrier Local SSA office
Hearing	6 months from receipt of review decision	Appellant	At least $100	File form SSA-1965 with local SSA office
ALJ		Appellant	At least $500	Same as Part A (see Table 6-2)
Federal District Court		Appellant	At least $1,000	Same as Part A (see Table 6-2)

*Section 9341 of OBRA-1986 made this level available for Part B claims.

Before OBRA, denials made due to "homebound" and "intermittent skilled care" were not protected under the provision of waiver of liability. Denials made on these bases between July 1, 1987, and September 30, 1989, are to be covered under waiver of liability provided the home health agency meets the following criteria:

• complies with requirements respecting timely submittal of bills for payment and medical documentation
• notifies patients and their physicians, where it is determined that a patient is being or will be furnished items or services which are excluded from coverage
• illustrates a favorable presumptive status for the previous quarter based on homebound or intermittent nursing care requirements.

The fiscal intermediary maintains specified data for each home health agency to determine the presumptive status. All visits that are billed as covered prior to a terminating event and excluding "grace day" visits are

Who Makes Decision	Time Limit for Decision	Documentation Required	Notice	Next Level
Insurance carrier	None	Original document Additional summary	Appellant	Hearing
Hearing officer designated by carrier	None	Same as review New evidence Oral argument	Appellant	Administrative Law Judge (ALJ)
ALJ	None	Same as Part A (see Table 6-2)	Appellant	Federal District Court
Court decision	None	Same as Part A (see Table 6-2)	Same as Part A	

divided by the number of visits determined by the home health agency to be covered but determined by the fiscal intermediary to be noncovered. The noncoverage determination may be based on either of the following reasons: (1) the services provided were not medically necessary and reasonable or constituted custodial care; or (2) the beneficiary was not homebound or did not need skilled care on an intermittent basis.

The provision under OBRA to protect technical denials with waiver of liability means two separate denial rate calculations are made.

Calculating Medical Necessity Denials

$$\frac{\text{All visits denied by the fiscal intermediary due to not medically necessary or reasonable or determined to be custodial care}}{\text{All visits the home health agency billed as covered}} = \text{Denial rate for medical necessity denials}$$

Calculating Technical Denials

$$\frac{\text{All visits denied by the fiscal intermediary due to homebound status or intermittent skilled need}}{\text{All visits the home health agency billed as covered}} = \text{Denial rate for technical denials}$$

In order for the home health agency to maintain a favorable presumptive status or waiver of liability, the denial rate cannot exceed 2.5 percent for the period being calculated.

Medical necessity denial rates are usually calculated on a calendar quarter but more frequently if the fiscal intermediary deems it necessary. Technical denials are calculated on a quarterly basis only. The home health agency is notified of its waiver of liability status by the end of the month following the end of the quarter or specified time period for which the denial rate was calculated (see HIM-11, Sections 260-265).

As a result, the home health agency has the potential for having a favorable presumptive status for both categories of denials, for only one category or for neither of the categories.

In view of coverage criteria and documentation issues, the "cushion" of waiver of liability may create an atmosphere in a home agency of accepting clients who are borderline as far as meeting coverage criteria. This may in turn dilute your skilled documentation. The home health agency's philosophy may become too liberal with its admission policies due to a dependence on the waiver of liability. It then may find itself with a denial rate in excess of 2.5 percent. This creates an unfavorable situation for the home health agency: it becomes eligible for a coverage compliance review; its denied claims are not appealable; it may lose its eligibility for PIP; and it may be placed on 100 percent medical review.

Again, the argument for prevention of denied claims outweighs the means to combat them. Chapters 4 and 5 of this text will assist health care professionals in the documentation of care provided. The thrust of this text concerns patient education but has a heavy emphasis on documentation, especially under the Medicare program. We believe these principles can be applied by any discipline and service area to improve continuity of patient care and enhance reimbursement from third party payors.

NOTES

1. D.J. Omdahl, "Preventing Home Care Denials," *American Journal of Nursing* 87, no. 8 (August 1987):1033.

2. D.M. Bumpass, "How Agencies Can Appeal Denied Medicare Claims," *Nursing & Health Care*, March 1982, pp. 134–137.

3. *Code of Federal Register* 51, no. 30 (February 13, 1986):5403–5412.

4. W.D. Cabin, *A Primer on the Medicare Claim Review and Denial Process for Home Care Providers*, 2nd ed. (Totowa, N.J.: William D. Cabin, 1987).

5. U.S. Department of Health and Human Services, *Medicare Intermediary Manual, Part 3: Claims Process*, Publication no. 13, Part 3, Section 2300 (Washington, D.C.: Health Care Financing Administration.

6. Cabin, *Primer on Medicare Claim Review and Denial Process*, pp. 31–32.

7. Ibid., p. 8.

8. Ibid., p. 9.

9. U.S. Department of Health and Human Services, *Home Health Agency Manual*, Publication no. 11, Sections 255-258, Interim Manual 86-5 (Washington, D.C.: Health Care Financing Administration, 1983).

10. *Home Health Line* 11 (1986):320.

BIBLIOGRAPHY

"Implementation of Home Health Prepayment Screening Module." *Regional Home Health Newsletter no. C87-06*. Medicare Administration Regional Home Health–New Mexico Blue Cross and Blue Shield, Inc., pp. 2–4.

National Association for Home Care. *HCFA Developing Standard National Screens for HHA Claims Processing*, Report no. 132. National Association for Home Care, 1985, p. 1.

Streimer, Robert A., Acting Director, Bureau of Eligibility, Reimbursement, and Coverage, Department of Health and Human Services, Health Care Financing Administration. Letter to Ms. Mary Townsend, Manager, Plan Performance and Assistance, Department of Operations, Blue Cross and Blue Shield Association, Chicago, Illinois, November 3, 1986. (Letter addressed Medicare Home Health coverage and reimbursement issues.)

U.S. Department of Health and Human Services. *Home Health Agency Manual*, Publication no. 11. Washington, D.C.: Health Care Financing Administration, 1983.

U.S. Department of Health and Human Services. *Medicare Carriers Manual, Part 2: Program Administration*, Publication no. 14, Part 2. Washington, D.C.: Health Care Financing Administration.

U.S. Department of Health and Human Services. *Medicare Intermediary Manual, Part 3: Claims Process*, Publication no. 13, Part 3. Washington, D.C.: Health Care Financing Administration.

Part III

Teaching Plans for the Home Care Patient

This part of the book was written to assist the nurse in developing teaching plans. In Chapters 7 through 13, sample teaching plans were formulated using seven common medical conditions seen by home health care professionals:

- cerebral vascular accident (CVA)
- malignant neoplasm
- diabetes mellitus, Type II
- arteriosclerotic heart disease
- acquired immune deficiency syndrome (AIDS)
- ventilator-dependent patient
- patient receiving parenteral medications.

Each of these chapters includes a brief discussion of the condition, assessment of the teaching needs related to the condition, nursing diagnoses related to the teaching needs, and a sample teaching care plan with sample documentation. At the end of each chapter, we provide a list of available resources pertinent to patient teaching for reference.

The conditions chosen are certainly not inclusive of problems dealt with in home health but represent some of the most frequently seen conditions, usually requiring a multidisciplinary approach and astute assessment and patient teaching by the nurse.

Included in the sample teaching plans are sample diagnoses, goals, and plans. They are intended to augment the development of a specific individualized teaching plan. They are in no way inclusive of all possible problems. It is the nurse's responsibility to develop an individualized teaching plan based on assessment and should become an integral part of the patient's multidisciplinary care and medical record. See Appendix C for an assessment, teaching care plan, and documentation guide. The nurse should realize that visit frequency must be based on the patient's overall assessment and needs, not just the teaching needs, as addressed here.

Throughout these chapters, the terms "family," "significant other," and "caregiver" are used synonymously. They identify the person who is directly responsible for the patient's care and to whom the patient teaching will be addressed if necessary.

Chapter 7

The Patient with a Cerebral Vascular Accident

Objectives

- To discuss briefly statistics, pathophysiology and signs and symptoms of cerebral vascular accident.
- To describe the assessment data needed to teach the patient with a cerebral vascular accident.
- To identify nursing diagnoses related to the teaching needs of a patient with a cerebral vascular accident.
- To provide a sample teaching plan for a patient with a cerebral vascular accident including nursing diagnosis, learning objective, plan, and teaching methods.
- To provide a sample documentation guide for a patient with a cerebral vascular accident addressing the nursing diagnoses identified in the teaching plan.

7

THE CONDITION

Cerebral vascular accident (CVA) is the most common disease of the nervous system. It is the third highest cause of death and the second cause of chronic disability and illness in the United States.[1]

A CVA is described as a pathologic condition in which there is occlusion of the cerebral blood vessels. The three major causes of this event are thrombus, embolus, or hemorrhage.[2] When any of these occurs, there is ischemia of the area of the brain normally perfused by the damaged vessels. When ischemia occurs, there is a disruption of cellular metabolism. Cell death can occur in 3 to 10 minutes. Permanent cell damage results in a cerebral infarction, which is accompanied by cerebral edema that further worsens the neurologic deficits.

The neurologic deficits that develop will depend on the location of the CVA and the severity of the cerebral edema. The middle cerebral artery is the most frequently affected, and this can leave the patient with both motor and sensory deficits contralateral to the lesion that include aphasia, homonymous hemianopsia, paralysis, apraxia, agnosia, and paralysis of conjugate gaze. The second most affected vessel is the internal carotid artery; this can also leave the patient with both motor and sensory deficits contralateral to the lesion. Clinical manifestations include all of those associated with damage to the middle cerebral artery and ipsilateral blindness.

There are many risk factors related to CVA. The major of these is hypertension. Other risk factors include diabetes; cardiac disease; elevated serum cholesterol, lipoproteins, and triglycerides; obesity; sedentary life style; smoking; and stress.

ASSESSMENT OF TEACHING NEEDS RELATED TO THE CONDITION

The usual length of hospital stay for the patient with a CVA is 9.9 days according to its diagnosis-related group.[3] When the patient is discharged to home, there are usually many teaching concerns to be considered along with multiple other problems the patient and significant others will face in the days to follow. A thorough assessment of the patient and his family should take place as soon as possible. The patient has teaching needs that are often best assessed through a multidisciplinary conference. The patient's needs will vary greatly depending on the amount of cerebral damage and resulting deficits.

When assessing the patient's teaching needs, recall the areas to assess: educational needs, learner readiness, and the teaching situation. The following areas should be considered in assessing the patient's and family's educational needs:

- Does the patient and family know the diagnosis and prognosis and understand the disease process?
- Can the patient understand his illness and recognize its impact on the future?

The patient and/or family should be questioned concerning the prescribed medical regimen, including diet, medication, and activity; their understanding of it; and how important they believe it to be in realizing the patient's rehabilitation potential. Knowledge of risk factors related to CVA should be assessed as well as the ability to recognize signs and symptoms of an impending CVA.

The nurse, patient, and family should identify temporary or permanent neurologic deficits for which the patient may need to compensate. These may include but are not limited to

- speech deficits
- emotional lability

- difficulty generalizing
- paralysis
- homonymous hemianopsia.

If the patient has deficits in these areas, further questions should ensue. For instance, if the patient has paralysis, there is no need to assess further the severity of the paralysis. If the patient is unable to provide self-care, it is necessary to assess the family's knowledge of range of motion exercises, proper positioning, turning, and bathing of the patient.

The need for assistive devices and knowledge related to their use should be assessed. The patient's and family's knowledge regarding the provision of a safe environment should be assessed. As stated earlier, assessment of educational needs depends on the neurologic deficits present. These are essential areas of assessment in formulating the teaching plan, but the nurse should use her judgment in individualizing her assessment of each patient.

The patient's and family's readiness to learn is the second part of assessment. This depends greatly on the severity of the neurologic deficits present and how capable the patient is of understanding the full impact of his illness and his physical and mental ability to learn. The patient who has visual disturbances is obviously not able to use written material in his learning, and it would be difficult for the aphasic patient to communicate his knowledge of medications.

With many CVA patients, some other person becomes the primary caregiver; thus the importance of assessing the readiness to learn of caregivers should be recognized. Are they capable of learning the information necessary to care for the patient? Are they unable to learn due to nonacceptance of the patient's condition, their own physical or mental inability, or their unwillingness to take on what is often an overwhelming and exhausting job? The readiness of both the patient and family is important in assessing the teaching needs of the patient.

The teaching situation is an essential component of patient learning and must be carefully assessed. Does the patient have the mental and physical ability to learn? Do his family members? Is there a family member available and willing to take on the responsibility of a caregiver?

In addition to assessing the resources available in the home, the nurse should explore with the patient and family the professional and community resources available for the patient. These might include local support groups, Meals on Wheels, social and financial services, and local service groups that can help obtain assistive devices. Through the assessment of these three areas, the teaching needs of the patient with a CVA can be better recognized and an effective teaching plan formulated.

NURSING DIAGNOSES RELATED TO TEACHING NEEDS

After assessing the patient's teaching needs, the nurse can formulate a nursing diagnosis or diagnoses. The diagnostic category of knowledge deficit would be chosen from 72 approved diagnostic categories (see Appendix B). In choosing the category, the nurse is confirming an actual need for knowledge and/or instruction. The latter part of the statement would indicate the areas in which the patient needs instruction (see Exhibit 2-1).

In reference to a CVA patient, there are many areas in which a knowledge deficit may exist. They may include

- condition
- risks
- medical regimen
- nutritional requirements
- use of assistive devices
- inability to provide self-care
- community services.

Examples of possible nursing diagnoses are

- knowledge deficit related to poor understanding of medical regimen
- knowledge deficit related to identification of signs and symptoms of impending CVA
- knowledge deficit related to inability to provide self-care
- knowledge deficit related to inability to use assistive devices, e.g., wheelchair
- knowledge deficit related to patient's inability to communicate with family due to his aphasia.

For the purpose of this discussion, three nursing diagnoses are identified. When considering how different each CVA patient can be, it should be recognized that the diagnoses can be few or many. From these diagnoses, the nurse formulates the teaching plan, including patient goals. See Appendix C for guides assisting the nurse in assessing the patient's teaching needs, developing a teaching plan, and documenting the plan after implementation.

SAMPLE TEACHING PLAN

Exhibit 7-1 is a sample teaching plan for CVA patients.

SAMPLE DOCUMENTATION GUIDES

Nursing Diagnosis: Knowlege Deficit Related to Poor Understanding of Medical Regimen

Nursing Diagnosis Addressed	Knowledge deficit related to poor understanding of medical regimen
Teaching Directed To	Patient and significant other
Learning Enhancements/ Barriers	1. Patient has right-sided weakness (B) 2. Intermittent lapses of memory (B) 3. Slurred speech (B) 4. Daughter staying with patient, very supportive and willing to learn (E)
Method of Teaching	L and P (see Exhibit 7-1 for codes)
Instruction	Instructed patient in prescribed medications: 1. name of drug: Coumadin (warfarin sodium): to take at same time every day (preferably in evening) 2. indirectly interferes with blood clotting, deters further extension of existing

Note: (B) Barriers
(E) Enhancements

Exhibit 7-1 Sample Teaching Plan: CVA

Patient's Name _____

Nursing Diagnosis	Learning Objectives	Plan	Teaching Method*	Date Plan Established	Initials
Knowledge deficit related to poor understanding of medical regimen	The patient will identify the components of the medical regimen.	Instruct in: medications: trade/generic name, use, side effects, dosage, and time.	L, P, C	3/11/87	E. J., R.N.
Knowledge deficit related to identification of signs and symptoms of impending CVA	The patient will identify signs and symptoms to report to the nurse or physician.	Instruct in: 1. increased weakness or loss of sensation in extremities 2. increase in visual disturbances 3. increased lethargy, irritability, or confusion 4. increased difficulty in swallowing 5. increased difficulty in communication 6. loss of consciousness 7. seizures.	L, G, P, M	3/11/87	E. J., R.N.
Knowledge deficit related to inability to provide self-care	The patient/significant other will demonstrate the proper methods of providing personal care to patient.	Instruct in: 1. bed bath 2. turning/positioning 3. range of motion exercises 4. personal care, i.e., skin care, oral hygiene, etc.	L, G, D, R, P, M	3/11/87	E. J., R.N.

*Method of teaching codes: L = lecture; G = group discussion; D = demonstration; R = role playing; P = programmed instruction; C = contracts; M = media.

clots, and prevents new clots from forming

3. side effects: bleeding, anorexia, nausea, vomiting, dermatitis if hypersensitive to drug
4. dosage individualized according to pro-thrombin time response
5. instructed patient and caregiver impor-tance of taking med every day. *Do not skip a dose.* Take at same time every day, preferably in PM.[4]

Evaluation of Learning

1. Patient's attention span was very short. Unable to repeat precautions.
2. Directed dosage, time, uses, side effects, and precautions to daughter. Left her with written teaching plan. Questioned me several times concern-ing the precautions.

Plan

Next visit will ask daughter and patient to demonstrate understanding of teaching today. Will begin instructions in signs and symptoms of impending CVA.

Nursing Diagnosis: Knowledge Deficit Related to Identification of Signs and Symptoms of Impending CVA

Nursing Diagnosis Addressed

Knowledge deficit related to identification of signs and symptoms of impending CVA

Teaching Directed To

Patient and significant other

Learning Enhancements/ Barriers

1. Patient has right-sided weakness (B)
2. Intermittent lapses of memory (B)
3. Slurred speech (B)
4. Daughter staying with patient, very supportive and willing to learn (E)

Method of Teaching	L and P (see Exhibit 7-1 for codes)
Instruction	1. Instructed patient in the following signs and symptoms of an impending CVA. (See teaching plan in Exhibit 7-1.) 2. Left list of signs and symptoms with patient and daughter.
Evaluation of Learning	1. Patient and daughter were very attentive. Patient has just gotten up from afternoon nap and was refreshed. Appeared to comprehend instructions. Was able to recite three of the seven signs and symptoms taught. 2. Instructed in precautions of Coumadin again; appeared to comprehend this visit. Daughter states patient is adhering to medication regimen without any evident side effects.
Plan	Next visit will instruct patient and significant other in self-care and/or assistance of caregiver in personal care.

Nursing Diagnosis: Knowledge Deficit Related to Inability to Provide Self-Care

Nursing Diagnosis Addressed	Knowledge deficit related to inability to provide self-care
Teaching Directed To	Patient and significant other
Learning Enhancements/ Barriers	1. Patient has ride-sided weakness (B) 2. Intermittent lapses of memory (B) 3. Slurred speech (B) 4. Daughter staying with patient, very supportive and willing to learn (E)
Method of Teaching	L and D (see Exhibit 7-1 for codes)

Instruction	Instructed daughter in assisting patient with self-care, sponge bath, transfer in and out of tub.
Evaluation of Learning	Patient and daughter became very frustrated due to weakness of right hand and arm. Patient is right-handed. Has difficulty using left hand. Daughter is leaving next week to return to her home. Patient became fatigued and had to lie down.
Plan	Contact physician for home health aide 2 × week and consult with occupational therapist concerning activity of daily living training and self-care instruction.

NOTES

1. W. Phipps, B. Long, and N. Woods, eds., *Medical Surgical Nursing: Concepts and Clinical Practice* (St. Louis: C.V. Mosby Co., 1987).

2. J. Thompson, G. McFarland, J. Hirsh, S. Tucker, A. Bowers, *Clinical Nursing* (St. Louis: C.V. Mosby Co., 1986).

3. W. Phipps, B. Long, and N. Woods, *Medical Surgical Nursing*.

4. L.E. Gavoni and J.E. Hayes, *Drugs and Nursing Implications*, 5th ed. (Norwalk, Conn.: Appleton-Century-Crofts, 1985), pp. 1281–1285.

BIBLIOGRAPHY

Birmingham, J. *Home Care Planning Based on DRGs.* Bethany, Conn.: Fleschner Publishing Co., Philadelphia: J.B. Lippincott Co., 1986.

Cahill, M., ed. *Patient Teaching.* Springhouse, Penn.: Springhouse Corp., 1987.

Carpenito, L. *Nursing Diagnosis: Application to Clinical Practice.* Philadelphia: J.B. Lippincott Co., 1983.

Ciranowicz, M., Furan, C., Kupnick, S., Weiner, S., and Welsh, N., eds. *Patient Teaching Manual 1.* Springhouse, Penn.: Springhouse Corp., 1987.

Doenges, M. *Nursing Care Plans: Nursing Diagnosis in Planning Patient Care.* Philadelphia: F.A. Davis Co., 1984.

Dudas, S. "Nursing Diagnoses and Interventions for the Rehabilitation of the Stroke Patient." *Nursing Clinics of North America* 2 (1986):345–357.

Gould, J.E., and Wargo, J. *Home Health Nursing Care Plans.* Rockville, Md.: Aspen Publishers, Inc., 1987.

Horne, E. "Mobility Problems of the New Stroke Victim: Supporting the Carer." *Professional Nurse,* April 1, 1986, pp. 191–193.

Luckmann, J., and Sorensen, K. *Medical Surgical Nursing: A Psychophysiologic Approach*, 2nd ed. Philadelphia: W.B. Saunders Co., 1980.

Myco, F. "Stroke Patients: A New Way of Living." *Nursing Times* 14 (1986):24–27.

Neal, M., Cohen, P., and Cooper, P. *Nursing Care Planning Guides for Long-Term Care.* Monterey, Calif.: Wadsworth Health Sciences & Pacific Palisades, Calif.: NURSECO, Inc., 1981.

Phipps, W., Long, B., and Woods, N., eds. *Medical-Surgical Nursing: Concepts and Clinical Practice.* St. Louis: C.V. Mosby Co., 1987.

Skidmore-Roth, L., and Jaffe, M. *Medical-Surgical Nursing Care Plans.* Norwalk, Conn.: Appleton-Century-Crofts, 1986.

Sloane, P.D. "How to Maintain the Health of Independent Elderly." *Geriatrics* 10 (1984): 93–95, 99–100, 104.

Thompson, J., McFarland, G., Hirsch, J., Tucker, S., and Bowers, A. *Clinical Nursing.* St. Louis: C.V. Mosby Co., 1986.

Ulrich, S., Canale, S., and Wendell S. *Nursing Care Planning Guides: A Nursing Diagnosis Approach.* Philadelphia: W.B. Saunders Co., 1986.

Chapter 8

The Patient with a
Malignant Neoplasm

Objectives

- To discuss briefly statistics, pathophysiology and signs and symptoms of malignant neoplasm.
- To describe the assessment data needed to teach the patient with a malignant neoplasm.
- To identify nursing diagnoses related to the teaching needs of a patient with a malignant neoplasm.
- To provide a sample teaching plan for a patient with a malignant neoplasm including nursing diagnosis, learning objective, plan, and teaching methods.
- To provide a sample documentation guide for a patient with a malignant neoplasm addressing the nursing diagnoses identified in the teaching plan.

8

THE CONDITION

Cancer ranks second as the cause of death in the United States. Cancer affects one of four people and claims more than 350,000 lives per year.[1] It is a disease that has great psychologic, social, and economic impact on the patient and his family. There are many risk factors and contributing factors related to neoplasms. These include genetic factors, hormonal factors, precancerous lesions, chronic irritation, drug therapy, environmental factors, and health practices. Everyone should be aware of the seven warning signs of cancer:

> **C:** change in bowel and bladder habits
> **A:** a sore that does not heal
> **U:** unusual bleeding or discharge
> **T:** thickening or a lump in the breast or elsewhere
> **I:** indigestion or difficulty swallowing
> **O:** obvious changes in a wart or mole
> **N:** nagging cough or hoarseness

Neoplasms are defined as a state in which cells proliferate without organization and often without differentiation. Uninhibited growth, uncontrolled function, and uncontrolled mobility result due to the increased proliferation and lack of differentiation. These actions permit spread of the cancer to other parts of the body via the blood and/or lymphatic system.[2,3] Cancers are classified into four major types: carcinomas, sarcomas, lymphomas, and leukemias.

In the early stages of a malignant neoplasm, there are usually few, if any, symptoms. As the neoplasm grows, one or several of the following problems can occur:

- Pressure upon surrounding organs
- Distortion of surrounding tissues
- Obstruction of lumens or tubes
- Interference with the blood supply of surrounding tissues
- Interference with organ function
- Disturbances of body metabolism
- Parasitic use of the body's nutritional supplies
- Mobilization of the body's defensive responses, resulting in inflammatory changes.[4]

Many clinical manifestations may result from pathologic changes. Local changes can cause obstruction, atrophy, ulceration, hemorrhage, or a secondary infection. Systemic changes can cause anemia, leukopenia, thrombocytopenia, infection, hemorrhage, weakness, cerebellar disease, pleural effusion, ascites, poor pulmonary function, and cachexia.

ASSESSMENT OF TEACHING NEEDS RELATED TO THE CONDITION

The length of hospital stay of patients with a malignant neoplasm varies according to the type of cancer, organ system affected, and mode of treatment. Due to the devastating effect of the diagnosis of cancer and the probable deterioration of the patient's condition, the patient and family will need ongoing assessment and evaluation of their teaching needs.

In caring for patients in the home, the nurse should have a strong knowledge base regarding the physiology of numerous cancers, patterns of metastasis, recommended treatment protocols, and their side effects. The nurse should have a good understanding of family counseling techniques, communication skills, ethics, management principles, psychosocial responses to illness, and available community resources. All of these become essential in assessing the teaching needs of the patient with a malignant neoplasm.

When assessing this patient and his family for teaching needs, recall areas to assess: educational needs, learner readiness, and the teaching situation. Due to the number of cancer diagnoses, a discussion of each primary cancer site is beyond the scope of this book. The discussion will address problems common to all patients with cancer.

To ensure that the cancer patient's physical needs are met after he returns home, the nurse must do a thorough assessment of the patient's and family's teaching needs. One must always keep in mind that the diagnosis of cancer can easily threaten one's sense of well-being. Patients diagnosed with cancer often have many misconceptions concerning the disease. These must be assessed in order to provide effective teaching. Some myths that are often believed are that cancer is always fatal, always excruciatingly painful, always mutilates the body, and is contagious.

Questions the nurse should ask during the assessment are

- Does the patient understand the disease process and his prognosis?
- Does he understand the treatment, which might include one or all of these: radiation, chemotherapy, or surgery?
- If the patient is receiving chemotherapy, does he understand the procedure and possible side effects? Does he know how to manage the side effects and prevent complications from developing?

Home care management also includes preventing protein-calorie malnutrition, which can lead to cachexia, and the prevention of infection, which can be so devastating to the cancer patient. If the patient is unable to provide self-care, the appointed caregiver's knowledge of providing care must be assessed. The condition of the patient with a malignant neoplasm can vary with each individual; the nurse must closely assess the patient and his family for their educational needs.

It is evident when one considers the psychological impact of the diagnosis of cancer how important learner readiness is to the teaching process. For the cancer patient, there may be many factors that affect learner readiness. These may include

- poor acceptance of the diagnosis by both the patient and family
- poor coping measures

- physical discomfort due to pain
- weakness
- nausea
- vomiting.

Many other problems may be present that affect the learner readiness of the patient and caregiver. The mental ability to learn must also be considered. Caregivers must recognize the stress-laden job they are undertaking. Their own physical and mental readiness to do this must be carefully assessed. Due to the impact of a diagnosis of cancer, learner readiness may take longer than it does with other conditions.

The teaching situation includes the home environment and those involved. Is the home environment set up so that those taught to provide care will be able to do so? Is the patient capable of being taught? If a family member is going to be the primary caregiver, is he or she available and willing to take on the responsibility?

The nurse should also discuss with the patient and family the professional and community resources available. These may include social services to help with financial matters and the local chapter of the American Cancer Society. If the patient is receiving only palliative treatment, the patient and family should be made aware of available hospice care. Many home health agencies provide hospice care. If yours does not, this would be an excellent area in which to work closely with the local hospice agency to provide a holistic approach for your patient.

As the patient and family are assessed, and teaching needs are established, the nurse can assist them in realizing that cancer is a disease that can be managed. Through patient teaching, many of the fears and misconceptions can be alleviated, and through the knowledge and skill learned, the patient can lead a more productive life.

NURSING DIAGNOSES RELATED TO TEACHING NEEDS

After establishing the patient's teaching needs, the nurse can formulate a nursing diagnosis or diagnoses. The diagnostic category of knowledge deficit would be chosen from the 72 approved diagnostic categories (see Appendix B). In choosing this category, the nurse is confirming an actual need for knowledge and/or instruction. The latter part of the statement would indicate the areas in which the patient needs instruction (see Exhibit 2-1).

When considering the patient with a malignant neoplasm, the following areas may be included:

- disease process
- misconceptions
- treatments
- management of side effects
- self-care management
- available resources.

Examples of possible diagnoses are

- knowledge deficit related to treatment with chemotherapy
- knowledge deficit related to management of side effects of chemotherapy, e.g., nausea, vomiting, mouth ulcers, hair loss
- knowledge deficit related to prevention of infection
- knowledge deficit related to prevention of protein-calorie malnutrition
- knowledge deficit related to available resources.

For the purpose of this discussion, three diagnoses are identified. The actual patient may have one or many diagnoses. From these diagnoses, the nurse formulates the teaching plan, including patient goals. See Appendix C for guides to assist the nurse in assessing the patient's teaching needs, developing a teaching plan, and documenting the plan after implementation.

SAMPLE TEACHING PLAN

A sample teaching plan for the cancer patient is shown in Exhibit 8-1.

Exhibit 8-1 Sample Teaching Plan: Malignant Neoplasm

Patient's Name

Nursing Diagnosis	Learning Objective	Plan	Teaching Method*	Date Plan Established	Initials
Knowledge deficit related to the management of side effects of chemotherapy (nausea, vomiting, mouth ulcers, hair loss)	Verbalize how to manage side effects of chemotherapy: mouth ulcers, hair loss, nausea, and vomiting.	Instruct in the following measures to control side effects: 1. Mouth ulcers a. avoid foods that are difficult to chew b. eat soft, bland food c. maintain good oral hygiene.	L, G, P	3/11/87	E. J., R.N.
		2. Hair loss a. hair styled to minimize hair loss b. wash gently with mild shampoo c. use wig, hat, etc.	L		
		3. Nausea and vomiting a. eat small, frequent meals b. avoid lying down c. take antiemetics as prescribed.	L, G, P		
Knowledge deficit related to prevention of infection	The patient will identify three ways to prevent infection.	1. Explain why the patient has lowered resistance when white blood count is down.	L, P	3/11/87	E. J., R.N.

			Method of teaching*	Date	Initials
		2. Instruct the patient in ways to prevent infection: a. adequate rest b. high-calorie, protein-rich diet c. avoid exposure to persons with infections.	L, P, M		
Knowledge deficit related to the prevention of protein-calorie malnutrition	The patient will identify three ways to prevent protein-calorie malnutrition.	Instruct in the following: 1. Explain what protein-calorie malnutrition is.	L, P	3/11/87	E. J., R.N.
		2. Identify signs and symptoms of protein-calorie malnutrition: a. weight loss b. muscle wasting c. apathy/lethargy.	L, P, G		
		3. Instruct in measures to prevent protein-calorie malnutrition: a. well-balanced diet b. ways to stimulate appetite c. how to cope with problems that may contribute to poor appetite.	L, G, P, M		

*Method of teaching codes: L = lecture; G = group discussion; D = demonstration; R = role playing; P = programmed instruction; C = contracts; M = media.

SAMPLE DOCUMENTATION GUIDES

Nursing Diagnosis: Knowledge Deficit Related to Management of Side Effects of Chemotherapy

Nursing Diagnosis Addressed	Knowledge deficit related to management of side effects of chemotherapy (nausea, vomiting, mouth ulcers, hair loss)
Teaching Directed To	Patient and significant other
Learning Enhancements/ Barriers	1. Patient very ill due to chemotherapy (B) 2. Wife upset: cries intermittently due to diagnosis of cancer (B) 3. Patient worried about financial obligations (B)
Method of Teaching	L, D, P (see Exhibit 8-1 for codes)
Instruction	1. Instructed patient and wife in soft foods that are high in protein/calories, i.e., milk shakes, malts, Instant Breakfast with eggs, milk, and ice cream. 2. Instructed wife to mash or blend foods. 3. Instructed patient to clean teeth and rinse mouth with a diluted mouthwash. 4. Instructed wife in proper administration of prescribed antiemetic, i.e., rectal insertion. Give every 6 hours as ordered if patient needs it. Try to give 30 to 40 minutes before a meal to enhance patient's appetite.
Evaluation of Learning	Patient is too ill to comprehend teaching this visit. Wife comprehended teaching fairly well, but is very emotional when patient becomes ill. She fears patient will

Note: (B) Barriers
    (E) Enhancements

become dependent on drugs and is not administering antiemetic as often as ordered by physician.

Plan

1. Contact physician for mouth rinse to relieve discomfort.
2. Obtain order for medical social worker.
3. Teach other measures to manage side effects of chemotherapy not covered today.
4. Begin instruction in protein-calorie malnutrition due to nausea, vomiting, and lack of appetite. Weight loss this week 2 lb.

Nursing Diagnosis: Knowledge Deficit Related to Prevention of Infection

Nursing Diagnosis Addressed

Knowledge deficit related to prevention of infection

Teaching Directed To

Patient and significant other

Learning Enhancements/ Barriers

1. Patient sitting up; appears to be feeling better (E)

Method of Teaching

L, P (see Exhibit 8-1 for codes)

Instruction

1. Instructed in reasons patient's resistance is low.
2. Written instruction sheet left with patient and significant other: "Ways to Prevent Infection."

Evaluation of Learning

Patient did not fully understand reasons for his susceptibility to infection.

Plan

Wife and patient to demonstrate knowledge of "Ways to Prevent Infection" as listed on instruction sheet next visit. Begin protein-calorie malnutrition instruction.

Nursing Diagnosis: Knowledge Deficit Related to Prevention of Protein-Calorie Malnutrition

Nursing Diagnosis Addressed	Knowledge deficit related to the prevention of protein-calorie malnutrition
Teaching Directed To	Patient and significant other
Learning Enhancements/ Barriers	1. Patient sleeping most of the day, wife states (B) 2. Wife much calmer and appears less stressed than last visit (E)
Method of Teaching	L and P (see Exhibit 8-1 for codes)
Instruction	1. Instructed in reasons for protein-calorie malnutrition. Written instruction sheet given: "Protein-Calorie Malnutrition." Instructed in major points wife should be aware of and concerned about. 2. Instructed in signs and symptoms of protein-calorie malnutrition as identified in teaching plan. 3. Instructed in a well-balanced diet, i.e., food groups, menu planning, several small meals a day, etc. 4. Instructed in ways to stimulate appetite, i.e., administering antiemetic 30 minutes before a meal, small and frequent meals, etc. 5. Instructed in ways to cope with problems that contribute to poor appetite; written instruction sheet left with wife. **Note:** These instructions would not be taught in one visit. Depending on the pa-

tient and/or the wife's comprehension, it could take several visits to complete the teaching of one area.

Evaluation of Learning

1. Wife was able to repeat major points of "Protein-Calorie Malnutrition" handout.
2. Wife was able to identify signs and symptoms readily, as patient is beginning to exhibit weight loss and muscle wasting.
3. Wife has a good understanding of a well-balanced diet but lacks knowledge in 4 and 5 above.

Plan

1. Instruct next visit in ways to stimulate appetite (bring written handout).
2. Medical social worker to visit tomorrow; will confer with her. Explained reason for visit to wife.

NOTES

1. R. McCorckle and B. Germino, "What Nurses Need to Know about Home Care," *Oncology Nursing Forum* 11, no. 6 (November/December 1984):63–69.

2. W. Phipps, B. Long, and N. Woods, eds., *Medical Surgical Nursing: Concepts and Clinical Practice* (St. Louis: C.V. Mosby Co., 1987).

3. J. Thompson, G. McFarland, J. Hirsch, S. Tucker, and A. Bowers, *Clinical Nursing* (St. Louis: C.V. Mosby Co., 1986).

4. J. Luckman and K. Sorensen, *Medical-Surgical Nursing: A Psychophysiologic Approach*, 2nd ed. (Philadelphia: W.B. Saunders Co., 1980).

BIBLIOGRAPHY

Birmingham, J. *Home Care Planning Based on DRGs*. Bethany, Conn.: Fleschner Publishing Co., Philadelphia: J.B. Lippincott Co., 1986.

Cahill, M., ed. *Patient Teaching*. Springhouse, Penn.: Springhouse Corp., 1987.

Carpenito, L. *Nursing Diagnosis: Application to Clinical Practice*. Philadelphia: J.B. Lippincott Co., 1983.

Ciranowicz, M., Furan, C., Kupnick, S., Weiner, S., and Welsh, N., eds. *Patient Teaching Manual 1*. Springhouse, Penn.: Springhouse Corp., 1987.

Dodd, M. "Self-Care for the Side Effects in Cancer Chemotherapy and Radiation Therapy." *AARN Newsletter* 43, no. 2 (February 1987):11–12.

Dodd, M.J. "Self-Care for Side Effects in Cancer Chemotherapy: An Assessment of Nursing Intervention: Part II." *Cancer Nursing* 1, no. 6 (1983):63–67.

Doenges, M. *Nursing Care Plans: Nursing Diagnosis in Planning Patient Care.* Philadelphia: F.A. Davis Co., 1984.

Dwyer, J. "Nutrition Education of the Cancer Patient and Family: Myths and Realities." *Cancer* 58 (Suppl. 8) (1986):1887–1896.

Fredette, S.L., and Beattie, H.M. "Living with Cancer: A Patient Education Program." *Cancer Nursing* 9, no. 6 (December 1986):308–316.

Germino, B., and McCorckle, R. "What Nurses Need to Know about Home Care." *Oncology Nursing Forum* 11, no. 6 (November/December 1984):63–69.

Glanz, K. "Nutrition Education for Risk Factor Reduction and Patient Education: A Review." *Preventative Medicine* 6, no. 14 (November 1985):721–752.

Gould, J.E., and Wargo, J. *Home Health Nursing Care Plans.* Rockville, Md.: Aspen Publishers, Inc., 1987.

Grant, M.M. "Nutritional Interventions: Increasing Oral Intake." *Seminar Oncology Nurse* 1, no. 2 (February 1986):36–43.

Fanslow, J. "Guidelines for Nursing Care of Patients with a Knowledge Deficit." *Oncology Nurse Forum* 3, no. 10 (Summer 1983):98–100.

Jaffe, M., and Skidmore-Roth, L. *Medical-Surgical Nursing Care Plans.* Norwalk, Conn.: Appleton-Century-Crofts, 1986.

Kramer, R.F., and Perin, G. "Patient Education and Pediatric Oncology." *Nursing Clinics of North America* 20, no. 1 (March 1985):31–48.

Luckmann, J., and Sorensen, K. *Medical Surgical Nursing: A Psychophysiologic Approach*, 2nd ed. Philadelphia: W.B. Saunders Co., 1980.

Neal, M., Cohen, P., and Cooper, P. *Nursing Care Planning Guides for Long-Term Care.* Monterey, Calif.: Wadsworth Health Sciences & Pacific Palisades, Calif.: NURSECO, Inc., 1981.

Phipps, W., Long, B., and Woods, N., eds. *Medical-Surgical Nursing: Concepts and Clinical Practice.* St. Louis: C.V. Mosby Co., 1987.

Richardson, E.A. "When Cancer Treatment Causes Hair Loss." *RN* 12 (1986):24–25.

Rimer, B., Jones, E.L., Keintz, M.K., Catolano, R.B., and Engstrom, P.F. "Informed Consent: A Crucial Step in Cancer Patient Education." *Health Education Quorum* (Suppl. 10) (Spring 1984):30–42.

Thompson, J., McFarland, G., Hirsch, J., Tucker, S., and Bowers, A. *Clinical Nursing.* St. Louis: C.V. Mosby Co., 1986.

Ulrich, S., Canale, S., and Wendell, S. *Nursing Care Planning Guides: A Nursing Diagnosis Approach.* Philadelphia: W.B. Saunders Co., 1986.

Welch-McCaffrey, D. "Evolving Patient Education Needs in Cancer." *Oncology Nurse Forum* 5, no. 12 (September/October 1985):62–66.

Welch-McCaffrey, D. "To Teach or Not to Teach? Overcoming Barriers to Patient Education in Geriatric Oncology." *Oncology Nurse Forum* 4, no. 13 (July/August 1987):25–31.

Wood, H.A. "Nutritional Teaching Cards." *Oncology Nurse Forum* 3, no. 12 (1985):71–74.

Chapter 9

The Patient with Diabetes Mellitus

Objectives

- To discuss briefly statistics, pathophysiology and signs and symptoms of diabetes mellitus.
- To describe the assessment data needed to teach the patient with diabetes mellitus.
- To identify nursing diagnoses related to the teaching needs of a patient with diabetes mellitus.
- To provide a sample teaching plan for a patient with diabetes mellitus including nursing diagnosis, learning objective, plan, and teaching methods.
- To provide a sample documentation guide for a patient with diabetes mellitus addressing the nursing diagnoses identified in the teaching plan.

9

THE CONDITION

Diabetes mellitus is one of the most common endocrine diseases. It is the third leading cause of death by disease in the United States and decreases the average life expectancy by one third. Every year, more than 250,000 new cases of diabetes are diagnosed.[1] There is no single definition for diabetes mellitus. It is a complex, chronic disorder in which there is a disruption of normal carbohydrate, fat, and protein metabolism. As the disease progresses, microvascular, macrovascular, and neuropathies develop. Diabetes mellitus has two types: insulin dependent diabetes mellitus (IDDM or Type I) and non-insulin dependent diabetes (NIDDM or Type II). Type I diabetes usually occurs in children but can occur at any age. Type II diabetes accounts for 80 percent of all cases. Factors contributing to this include age, obesity, and heredity.

In Type I diabetes, there is usually an absolute deficiency in insulin secretion, which results from destruction of the beta cells of the pancreas caused by a virus or autoimmune disorder. It is believed that this destruction occurs as mononuclear cells progressively infiltrate the pancreas. The body's ability to maintain normal blood sugar levels deteriorates as the beta cells are destroyed.

In all types of diabetes, there is a relative insulin deficiency. Insulin levels may be depressed, normal, or high. The deficiency is thought to be caused by one or a combination of the following factors:

- reduced number of cellular insulin receptors
- decreased affinity of the insulin receptors
- possible islet cell defect
- lack of intracellular activation necessary for normal cell stimulation.

When an insulin deficiency exists, glucose cannot be used by the cells for energy metabolism. The resulting accumulation of glucose in the blood causes glucose to spill in the urine; fats and proteins are mobilized to provide energy; and the liver becomes less efficient in converting these acids to ketones; thus an acidotic state results. These metabolic derangements result in a number of clinical manifestations.[2–4]

Clinical manifestations may vary, depending on the disease. Some Type II diabetic patients may not present with symptoms until they have developed complications. The classic manifestations of Type I diabetes are polyuria, polydypsia, and polyphagia. Other manifestations of both types include weight loss, weakness, lethargy, hyperglycemia, neuropathies, retinopathy, nephropathy, and accelerated atherosclerosis.

The patient seen in the home may have either Type I or Type II diabetes. The majority of patients usually have Type II. The discussion that follows deals with assessing the learning needs of the diabetic patient (Type I or II) concerning diet, medications, and exercise.

ASSESSMENT OF TEACHING NEEDS RELATED TO THE CONDITION

Assessing the teaching needs of the diabetic patient is a vital component of his care. The outcome of this major health problem almost completely depends on the patient's self-management. Through the nurse's teaching, the patient is assisted in gaining the necessary knowledge, skills, and attitudes to manage his illness. The mean length of stay in the hospital for the patient with diabetes ranges from 5.6 to 7.7 days, depending on the age of the patient according to its diagnosis-related group.[5]

In this short time, the patient is instructed in many areas of care and has very little time to assimilate this information. Upon returning to his home, the diabetic patient takes this large amount of new knowledge and new skills, which he is expected to incorporate immediately into his life style. Even though teaching is begun in the hospital, home care follow-up is essential to the patient's success in obtaining independence in self-care. This knowledge and these skills are essential to the maintenance of his health.

When assessing the patient's teaching needs, recall the three areas to assess: educational needs, learner readiness, and available resources. There are many areas to be considered when assessing the patient with diabetes. Do the patient and family understand the disease process and recognize the relation of good diabetic control and health? It is often difficult for the newly diagnosed diabetic patient to conceive that complications of neuropathies, retinopathy, or nephropathy could actually occur. The medical regimen, including diet, medications, and exercise, usually brings forth quite a change in the patient's life style and requires new knowledge and skills to achieve compliance.

Dietary management of diabetes with the use of exchange lists often appears very complex to the patient. Medication management, including insulin administration, certainly requires new skills and knowledge of the patient or family member.

The patient's ability to manage these two areas should be carefully assessed:

- Are the menus prepared by the patient or family member correct or is additional teaching needed?
- Can they demonstrate accurate dosage and correct insulin administration?
- Does the patient understand his exercise program and how it relates to diabetic control?
- Can they demonstrate blood and urine testing?
- Would the patient be able to recognize signs and symptoms of hypoglycemia and hyperglycemia and know what to do for each?
- Does the patient understand what sick-day precautions are?
- Can they demonstrate good skin and foot care measures, and do they recognize the importance of such care?
- Do they know the community resources available?

Other questions that should be asked relate to the patient's understanding of preventative measures related to reducing the risks of long-term complications and assessing the patient's and family's teaching needs. The readiness of the learner, as always, is an important component of the teaching assessment. Does the patient accept his illness and recognize the need for life style changes? Does he believe these changes are beneficial? Is the patient ready to administer insulin to himself? If not, is there someone else who is willing to learn and ready to accept such responsibility? Learner readiness will depend heavily on the patient's age. One might be dealing with a very young child and parent or an elderly patient with additional medical problems. Through careful assessment of learner readiness, the nurse can plan teaching sessions to meet the needs of the patient.

The teaching situation, which includes the environment and available resources, can have a great impact on the diabetic patient's learning. Is the environment suitable for teaching? Are there adequate resources? Are there family members available to offer support and provide care? If the family members are willing to do so, are they capable, both mentally and physically, of doing so?

The nurse should also explore with the patient and family the professional community resources available to them. A dietary consultant may be very beneficial in helping the patient manage his diet. Local civic groups may offer help in providing supplies, such as insulin syringes. Local chapters of the American Diabetic Association may also offer help. All of these can ease the transition of managing diabetes.

NURSING DIAGNOSES RELATED TO TEACHING NEEDS

After identifying the patient's teaching needs, the nurse can formulate a nursing diagnosis or diagnoses. The diagnostic category of knowledge deficit would be chosen from the 72 approved categories (see Appendix B). In choosing the category, the nurse is confirming an actual need for knowledge and/or instruction. The latter part of the statement would indicate the areas in which the patient needed instruction (see Exhibit 2-1).

Areas in which there may be a knowledge deficit for the diabetic patient include

- disease process
- nutrition
- exercise
- medications

- foot and skin care
- blood and urine testing
- signs and symptoms of hypoglycemia and hyperglycemia
- safety precautions
- illness
- community resources.

Examples of possible nursing diagnoses are

- knowledge deficit related to insulin injections
- knowledge deficit related to signs and symptoms of hypoglycemia and hyperglycemia
- knowledge deficit related to the role of exercise in diabetic management
- knowledge deficit related to foot care measures
- knowledge deficit related to dietary management.

For the purpose of this discussion, three diagnoses are identified. The needs of each patient will vary as will the number and kinds of nursing diagnoses. From the diagnoses, the nurse formulates a teaching plan, including patient goals. See Appendix C for guides assisting the nurse in assessing the patient's teaching needs, developing a teaching plan, and documenting the plan after implementation.

SAMPLE TEACHING PLAN

A sample teaching plan for the diabetic patient is shown in Exhibit 9-1.

SAMPLE DOCUMENTATION GUIDES

Nursing Diagnosis: Knowledge Deficit Related to Insulin Injections

Nursing Diagnosis Addressed	Knowledge deficit related to insulin injections
Teaching Directed To	Patient

Exhibit 9-1 Sample Teaching Plan: Diabetes Mellitus

Patient's Name _____

Nursing Diagnosis	Learning Objective	Plan	Teaching Method*	Date Plan Established	Initials
Knowledge deficit related to insulin injections	The patient will demonstrate self-administration of insulin.	Instruct in: 1. storage and care of insulin 2. injection technique 3. asepsis 4. site rotation 5. actions and side effects of the specific type of insulin prescribed 6. blood glucose monitoring according to type of monitor prescribed, i.e., Accucheck, Glucochek, Testape.	1. L, D, P 2. L, D, R, M 3. L, D, R, M 4. L, D, R, M 5. L, P 6. L, D, R, P, M	3/11/87	E. J., R.N.

		Instruct in:	L, P, M	3/11/87	E. J., R.N.
Knowledge deficit related to signs and symptoms of hypoglycemia and hyperglycemia	The patient will identify signs and symptoms of hypoglycemia and hyperglycemia.	1. factors that precipitate hypoglycemia or hyperglycemia 2. signs and symptoms of hypoglycemia or hyperglycemia 3. actions to take if either occurs.			
Knowledge deficit related to dietary management	Verbalize the principles of dietary management and prepare a sample menu.	Instruct in: 1. Review prescribed diet. 2. Discuss and explain exchange list and preselected menus. 3. Discuss and instruct in changes that must be made if meal schedule or activity changes significantly. 4. Assist with menu preparation.	1. L, P 2. L, D, P, M 3. L, P, M 4. L, G, D, R, P, C, M	3/11/87	E. J., R.N.

*Method of teaching codes: L = lecture; G = group discussion; D = demonstration; R = role playing; P = programmed instruction; C = contracts; M = media.

Learning Enhancements/ Barriers	1. Patient was upset due to insulin being prescribed (B). 2. Patient taught school for 20 years (E).
Method of Teaching	L, D, P (see Exhibit 9-1 for codes)
Instruction	Instructed in storage and care of insulin: 1. Store unused in refrigerator. 2. Vial in use should be at room temperature. 3. Discard opened vial if not used for several weeks. 4. Discard if outdated, discolored, or contains granules. 5. NPH insulin will have a precipitate and is cloudy when mixed. "Care and Storage of Insulin" handout left with patient. See attached.[6]
Evaluation of Learning	Patient reluctant to learn; stated: "If I don't learn I won't have to give my shots." Explained we would not be available on a daily basis forever. Became upset and cried.
Plan	Will ask for return demonstration tomorrow for comprehension of handout. Begin instruction.
Instruction	Instructed in: 1. drawing up insulin using aseptic technique 2. short video on "Injection Technique for Administration of Insulin."
Evaluation of Learning	She toyed with the insulin syringe; stated: "I really don't want to do this. They tried to

Note: (B) Barriers
(E) Enhancements

teach me in the hospital but I refused and that's why they sent me you."

Plan

Bring an orange and allow patient to draw up water and inject orange. Recall techniques in film.

Instruction

Demonstrated drawing up insulin, units on syringe, rotating vial to mix insulin, aseptic techniques. See attached handout: "Injection Techniques for Administration of Insulin."

Evaluation of Learning

Patient drew up water and injected orange. Did fairly well. Forgot to cleanse top of vial and area of injection on orange. Experienced difficulty obtaining the correct dosage on syringe.

Plan

Allow patient to draw up insulin for tomorrow's injection.

Instruction

Demonstrated aseptic technique before she drew up insulin.

Evaluation of Learning

Patient drew up insulin without incident. Very proud of herself. Asked if she could give her "shot." Had difficulty handling syringe with one hand. Assisted with injection.

Plan

Begin instruction in site rotation.

Instruction

Instructed in reasons for site rotation. Handout given.

Evaluation of Learning

Patient gave insulin injection today without incident. Very nervous. Trembling when finished. Had to sit for awhile before instructions could continue. Appeared to understand site rotations. Expressed concern she couldn't reach all areas.

Plan	Patient to demonstrate rotation tomorrow. Will observe.
Instruction	Observed patient's comprehension of site rotation
Evaluation of Learning	Demonstrated understanding self-administration of injection "perfect." Patient very proud; stated: "I really didn't think I could do this."
Plan	Begin instruction in NPH insulin next visit, i.e., action, side effects, etc.
Instruction	NPH insulin, 12 units/daily. Instructed in actions and side effects. "NPH-Insulin" handout given.
Evaluation of Learning	Patient appeared to comprehend instructions. Received some medication instruction in hospital.
Plan	Request patient to identify actions and side effects next visit and begin instruction in the glucose monitors.
Instruction	Instructed patient in use of glucose monitor and mechanics of machine. Booklet left with patient.
Evaluation of Learning	Patient was very cautious concerning the blood glucose monitor. Asked if she would have to stick herself again.
Plan	Instruct the blood glucose monitor in a step-by-step manner according to manufacturer's handbook.

Nursing Diagnosis: Knowledge Deficit Related to Signs and Symptoms of Hypoglycemia and Hyperglycemia

Nursing Diagnosis Addressed	Knowledge deficit related to signs and symptoms of hypoglycemia and hyperglycemia
Teaching Directed To	Patient
Method of Teaching	L, P, M, D (see Exhibit 9-1 for codes)
Instruction	Instructed in signs and symptoms of hypoglycemia since insulin is a factor that can precipitate it, i.e., fatigue, weakness, sweating, nervousness.
Evaluation of Learning	Patient concerned about hypoglycemia reaction. After questioning patient, discovered she drank only a glass of milk.
Plan	Patient is to record everything eaten in next 24 hours.
Instruction	Reviewed meal record; only 1,200 calories. Began instruction in exchange lists and counting calories.
Evaluation of Learning	Patient is skipping bread and some vegetables on menu. Did not understand how to substitute. Did not like some items on prepared menus.
Plan	Patient is to make a list of vegetables she likes; does not like bread. Will instruct in how to substitute.
Instruction	Instructed in actions to take. Due to NPH peak time, taught to eat afternoon snack and carry hard candy to treat a reaction. Handout "Hypoglycemia" given.

Evaluation of Learning   Patient more receptive today. Minister talked with her last evening. He also has insulin dependent diabetes. She was able to talk about her diabetes today without becoming upset. Was able to repeat the signs and symptoms of hypoglycemia and understood actions and side effects of NPH insulin. Did not remember reasons to discard insulin. Went over "Care and Storage of Insulin" again.

Plan   Begin instruction in 1,800-calorie ADA diet next visit.

Nursing Diagnosis: Knowledge Deficit Related to Dietary Management

Nursing Diagnosis Addressed   Knowledge deficit related to dietary management

Teaching Directed To   Patient

Learning Enhancements/ Barriers   Patient feeling better today (E)

Method of Teaching   L, P, M, D (see Exhibit 9-1 for codes)

Instruction   Instructed in counting 1,800 calories. Instructed in menu obtained in hospital.

Evaluation of Learning   Patient appears to understand counting of calories and appropriate measuring of food.

Plan   Instruct in exchange lists and begin menu planning.

Instruction	1. Instructed in exchange lists and how to substitute. 2. Assisted patient in preparing a menu from exchange lists of things she normally eats.
Evaluation of Learning	Patient understands exchange list but becomes confused when substituting anything not on her prepared menus from hospital. Was relieved she could prepare her own menus. Will need further instruction.
Plan	Patient is to prepare menus for Saturday and Sunday. I will review next visit.

Nursing Diagnosis: Knowledge Deficit Related to Dietary Management

Nursing Diagnosis Addressed	Knowledge deficit related to dietary management
Instruction	Reviewed the menus patient prepared. Minor adjustments required.
Evaluation of Learning	Patient is comprehending menu preparation with exchange lists. Did not include snacks.
Plan	Begin instruction in dietary adjustments next visit.
Instruction	1. Instructed in dietary adjustments required if ill, increased activity, or schedule changes. 2. Demonstrated changes on sample menu.

Evaluation of Learning	Patient became upset: "There is just too much to learn. I can't make these changes. I've just now understood how to use the exchange lists." Attempted to give patient too much information at once.
Plan	Will allow patient to absorb what has already been taught. Begin tomorrow with calculating dietary changes to make if ill and why.
Instruction	1. Instructed patient in increased need for carbohydrates and calories and the pathophysiology of why these needs occur. 2. Handout given: "Dietary Adjustments."
Evaluation of Learning	Patient more receptive today. Handout taught thoroughly. Stated she understood. "Everything is beginning to fall into place."
Plan	Instruct in dietary adjustments for increased activity and/or schedule changes.
Instruction	Instructed in dietary needs due to increased activity and/or schedule changes.
Evaluation of Learning	Patient had reviewed the handout on "Dietary Adjustments." She was much more relaxed and comprehended the instructions readily.
Plan	Evaluate comprehension of teaching to this point. Confer with other disciplines on this case. Revise teaching plan and care plan as necessary and reduce skilled nursing visits.

NOTES

1. R. McCorckle and B. Germino, "What Nurses Need to Know about Home Care," *Oncology Nursing Forum* 11, no. 6 (November/December 1984):63–69.

2. S. Ulrich, S. Canale, and S. Wendell, *Nursing Care Planning Guides: A Nursing Diagnosis Approach* (Philadelphia: W.B. Saunders Co., 1986).

3. W. Phipps, B. Long, and N. Woods, eds., *Medical-Surgical Nursing: Concepts and Clinical Practice* (St. Louis: C.V. Mosby Co., 1987).

4. J. Thompson, G. McFarland, J. Hirsch, S. Tucker, and A. Bowers, *Clinical Nursing* (St. Louis: C.V. Mosby Co., 1986).

5. H. Low, "Diabetes: Stable in the Community," *Community Outlook*, February 1985, pp. 27–31.

6. L.E. Govoni and J.E. Hayes, *Drugs and Nursing Implications*, 5th ed. (Norwalk, Conn.: Appleton-Century-Crofts, 1985), pp. 692–693.

BIBLIOGRAPHY

Birmingham, J. *Home Care Planning Based on DRGs.* Bethany, Conn.: Fleschner Publishing Co., Philadelphia: J.B. Lippincott Co., 1986.

Brown, S.A. "An Assessment of the Knowledge Base of the Insulin-Dependent Diabetic Adult." *Journal of Community Health Nursing* 1, no. 4 (1987):9–19.

Cahill, M., ed. *Patient Teaching.* Springhouse, Penn.: Springhouse Corp., 1987.

Carpenito, L. *Nursing Diagnosis: Application to Clinical Practice.* Philadelphia: J.B. Lippincott Co., 1983.

Casparie, A.F., and Elving, L.D. "Severe Hypoglycemia in Diabetic Patients: Frequency, Causes, Prevention." *Diabetes Care* 2, no. 8 (March-April 1985):141–145.

Ciranowicz, M., Furan, C., Kupnick, S., Weiner, S., and Welsh, N., eds., *Patient Teaching Manual 1.* Springhouse, Penn.: Springhouse Corp., 1987.

Doenges, M. *Nursing Care Plans: Nursing Diagnosis in Planning Patient Care.* Philadelphia: F.A. Davis Co., 1984.

Germer, S., Campbell, I.W., Smith A.W., Sutherland, J.D., and Jones, I.G. "Do Diabetics Remember All They Have Been Taught? A Survey of Knowledge of Insulin-Dependent Diabetics." *Diabetic Medicine* 4, no. 3 (July-August 1986):343–345.

Gould, J.E., and Wargo, J. *Home Health Care Plans.* Rockville, Md.: Aspen Publishers, Inc., 1987.

Jaffe, M., and Skidmore-Roth, L. *Medical-Surgical Nursing Care Plans.* Norwalk, Conn.: Appleton-Century-Crofts, 1986.

Jensen, M.D., and Miles, J.M. "The Roles of Diet and Exercise in the Management of Patients with Insulin-Dependent Diabetes Mellitus." *Mayo Clinic Proceedings* 10, no. 61 (October 1986):813–819.

Lorenz, R.A. "Training Health Professionals to Improve the Effectiveness of Patient Education Programs." *Diabetes Education* (Suppl. 12) (May 1986):204–209.

Low, H. "Diabetes: Stable in the Community." *Community Outlook*, February 1985, pp. 27–31.

Luckmann, J., and Sorensen, K. *Medical Surgical Nursing: A Psychophysiologic Approach*, 2nd ed. Philadelphia: W.B. Saunders Co., 1980.

Marynick, M.E., Kanwell, G.P., and Thomas, R.G. "A Test of Instruction Approaches Designed to Influence Food Selection." *Diabetes Education* 1, no. 12 (Winter 1986):24–27.

Miles, J.M., and Jensen, M.D. "Complications of Insulin-Dependent Diabetes Mellitus: Management of Insulin Reactions and Acute Illness." *Mayo Clinic Proceedings* 10, no. 61 (October 1986):820–824.

Most, R.S., Gross, A.M., Davidson, P.C., and Richardson, P. "The Accuracy of Glucose Monitoring by Diabetic Individuals in Their Home Setting." *Diabetes Education* 1, no. 12 (Winter 1986):24–27.

Neal, M., et al. *Nursing Care Planning Guides for Long-Term Care.* Monterey, Calif.: Wadsworth Health Sciences & Pacific Palisades, Calif.: NURSECO, Inc., 1981.

Phipps, W., Long, B., and Woods, N., eds. *Medical-Surgical Nursing: Concepts and Clinical Practice.* St. Louis: C.V. Mosby Co., 1987.

Robertson, C. "How to Teach Patients to Monitor Blood Glucose." *RN* 12, no. 48 (December 1985):24–25.

Sims, D.F. "Diabetes Patient Education: A Consumer View." *Diabetes Education* 2, no. 12 (Spring 1986):122–125.

"Teaching Your Patient about Blood Glucose Testing." *Nursing Life* 6, no. 5 (November/December 1985):41–42.

Thompson, J., McFarland, G., Hirsch, J., Tucker, S., and Bowers, A. *Clinical Nursing.* St. Louis: C.V. Mosby Co., 1986.

Ulrich, S., Canale, S., and Wendell, S. *Nursing Care Planning Guides: A Nursing Diagnosis Approach.* Philadelphia: W.B. Saunders Co., 1986.

Chapter 10

The Patient with a Myocardial Infarction

Objectives

- To discuss briefly statistics, pathophysiology and signs and symptoms of myocardial infarction.
- To describe the assessment data needed to teach the patient with myocardial infarction.
- To identify nursing diagnoses related to the teaching needs of a patient with myocardial infarction.
- To provide a sample teaching plan for a patient with myocardial infarction including nursing diagnosis, learning objective, plan, and teaching methods.
- To provide a sample documentation guide for a patient with myocardial infarction addressing the nursing diagnoses identified in the teaching plan.

10

THE CONDITION

Coronary heart disease is the leading cause of death in North America and Western Europe. It is estimated that 3.1 million Americans over 18 years old have coronary heart disease.[1] Coronary heart disease encompasses other conditions, but for the purpose of this text, home teaching of only the patient with a myocardial infarction (MI) is covered.

The exact cause of coronary heart disease is unknown, but the disease is associated with several predisposing risk factors. They include age, sex, race, family history, hypertension, high blood lipid levels, obesity, smoking, sedentary life style, stress, diabetes, and personality type. Some of these risk factors are modifiable; some are not. This is further discussed in the specific teaching plan.

As the disease develops, there is an accumulation of lipid and fibrous tissues within the coronary arteries, which can produce narrowing and occlusion. As the lumen narrows, the supply of blood flowing to the myocardium is reduced. With the decreased blood flow comes hypoxia to the myocardium, which can result in angina pectoris, MI, or sudden cardiac death. An MI is the result of severe ischemia to the myocardium caused by an interruption of coronary blood flow. When the occlusion occurs, there is a derangement of cellular electrolytes, lowered contractility, and attempts to compensate by the sympathetic nervous system.

145

Irreversible cellular damage and necrosis of cardiac muscle occur if the ischemia lasts longer than 35 to 45 minutes.[2]

The patient experiencing an MI may exhibit various clinical manifestations. Sudden, severe, crushing, substernal chest pain that may radiate to the neck, left arm, or right arm is the classic description of pain. Other manifestations include nausea, vomiting, indigestion, restlessness, fear of dying, shortness of breath, cyanosis, rales or rhonchi, increased heart rate, decreased blood pressure, and S_4 or S_3 heart sounds.

ASSESSMENT OF TEACHING NEEDS RELATED TO THE CONDITION

The mean length of stay in the hospital for a patient with an MI without complication is 9.8 days; with complications is 11.9 days. These are according to the diagnosis-related group.[3] No longer does the MI patient remain in the hospital 2 to 3 weeks. Thus, with early discharge, there is a need for patient teaching in the home and a thorough assessment of the patient's and his significant others' teaching needs.

When assessing the patient's teaching needs, keep in mind the three areas to assess: educational needs, learner readiness, and available resources. In assessing the patient's and significant other's educational needs, one must question:

- Does the patient understand the disease process and his prognosis?
- Does he understand the importance of the healing process?
- Could he recognize signs and symptoms of an extending or recurrent MI, and what signs and symptoms should he report to the physician?

It is assumed that these areas were addressed during hospitalization, but it is essential to assess the same areas in the patient's home environment. The patient's understanding of and ability to comply with the medical regime, including medications, diet, and activity, must be assessed. Can the patient identify risk factors, recognizing those that can be modified? Helping the patient modify these risk factors to reduce the chance of another MI is the primary goal of teaching the patient.[4] If the patient is to have his blood pressure and pulse taken regularly, have him or his significant other demonstrate the ability to do so. These were probably taught to the patient before discharge, but, all too often, skills taught in the hospital are forgotten once the patient returns home.

The readiness of the patient and the significant other to learn is vitally important to the assessment of teaching needs. With the MI patient, the continuation of learning to adhere to a medical regimen is often more difficult when he returns home. This is especially true if he feels good when he returns home. It is difficult for him to believe that he must not return to his past activity level or eating habits. His readiness to learn will depend greatly on how strongly he believes that compliance with his medical regimen will help him live a more healthy life. On the other hand, if the patient has returned home with very little cardiac reserve, he may not even be able to make it through brief teaching sessions. He is not ready to learn, and the teaching plan will have to be modified. Family members may not accept the patient's condition or have the ability to learn. All of these factors must be considered in assessing learner readiness.

The resources available to the patient must be assessed. Is there a strong support system in the home? Are family members available to help? Upon returning home, the spouse of the patient often has as much need for support as the patient. The nurse should also identify outside support for the family, such as local support groups and the local American Heart Association.

NURSING DIAGNOSES RELATED TO TEACHING NEEDS

The nurse should formulate a nursing diagnosis or diagnoses after assessing the patient's teaching needs. The diagnostic category of knowledge deficit would be chosen from the approved diagnostic categories (see Appendix B). In choosing this category, the nurse confirms the actual need for knowledge and/or instruction. The latter part of the diagnosis should identify areas of needed instruction (see Exhibit 2-1).

After assessing the patient, one might consider the following possible areas of knowledge deficits:

- disease etiology
- risk factors
- medication
- dietary instructions

- activity programs
- knowledge and skills needed for taking blood pressure and pulse
- signs and symptoms to report to the physician.

The following are examples of possible nursing diagnoses:

- knowledge deficit related to inability to identify signs and symptoms of an MI
- knowledge deficit related to poor understanding of prescribed medications
- knowledge deficit related to noncompliance with activity program.

For the purpose of this discussion, three diagnoses are identified. When one considers the individuality of each patient, it must be recognized that the diagnoses will vary for each. From these diagnoses, the nurse formulates the teaching plan, including patient goals. See Appendix C for guides assisting the nurse in assessing the patient's teaching needs, developing a teaching plan, and documenting the plan after implementation.

SAMPLE TEACHING PLAN

A sample teaching plan for the MI patient is shown in Exhibit 10-1.

SAMPLE DOCUMENTATION GUIDES

Nursing Diagnosis: Knowledge Deficit Related to Inability to Identify Signs and Symptoms of Myocardial Infarction

Nursing Diagnosis Addressed	Knowledge deficit related to inability to identify signs and symptoms of MI
Teaching Directed To	Patient and significant other
Learning Enhancements/ Barriers	1. Wife very supportive (E) 2. Patient: Type A personality (B)

Note: (B) Barriers
(E) Enhancements

Method of Teaching	L,P (see Exhibit 10-1 for codes)

Instruction   Instructed patient and wife in signs and symptoms to report to physician. Handout "Signs and Symptoms of an MI" left with patient.

Evaluation of Learning   Patient and wife very receptive to instruction. Patient still very weak but restless.

Plan   Begin instruction in medication next week.

Nursing Diagnosis: Knowledge Deficit Related to Poor Understanding of Medications

Nursing Diagnosis Addressed   Knowledge deficit related to poor understanding of medications

Teaching Directed To   Patient and significant other

Learning Enhancements/ Barriers
1. Wife very supportive (E)
2. Patient: Type A personality (B)

Method of Teaching   L, P (see Exhibit 10-1 for codes)

Instruction   **Note:** All new medications should be taught if patient and/or significant other exhibit a knowledge deficit of them. Each drug may necessitate a separate visit. Documentation should support this.

1. Instructed in medication:
   a. Name: digoxin
   b. Used to strengthen myocardial contraction; prevent congestive heart

Exhibit 10-1 Sample Teaching Plan: Myocardial Infarction

Patient's Name _____

Nursing Diagnosis	Learning Objective	Plan	Teaching Method*	Date Plan Established	Initials
Knowledge deficit related to inability to identify signs and symptoms of an MI	The patient will list four symptoms that should be reported to the physician.	Instruct the patient to report 1. chest pain, unrelieved by nitroglycerin 2. shortness of breath 3. nausea, vomiting 4. swelling 5. cold clammy skin 6. anxiety, restlessness 7. feeling of impending doom 8. dizziness 9. weakness.	L, G, R, P, M	3/18/87	E. J., R.N.
Knowledge deficit related to poor understanding of medications	The patient will identify all medications including use, side effects, dosage, and time.	Instruct in medications: 1. name 2. use 3. side effects 4. dosage 5. time.	L, P, C	3/18/87	E. J., R.N.
Knowledge deficit related to noncompliance with activity program	Comply with activity program and verbalize importance of doing so.	Review: 1. prescribed activity plan. 2. need for healing time of myocardium. 3. guidelines for sexual activity (be specific).	L, G, P, C, M	3/18/87	E. J., R.N.

*Method of teaching codes: L = lecture; G = group discussion; D = demonstration; R = role playing; P = programmed instruction; C = contracts; M = media.

failure, paroxysmal atrial tachycardia, atrial fibrillation, and flutter. Instructed wife in pulse taking techniques and when to hold medication if necessary.

c. Side effects are fatigue, generalized muscle weakness, agitation, hallucinations, arrhythmias, etc. Written handout with significant side effects and instructions to patient and significant other given.

d. Dose is 0.25 mg.

e. Take daily, usually in AM.[5]

Evaluation of Learning	Patient refuses medication at times, according to wife. He feels he is taking too much at times.
Plan	1. Instruct in pathophysiology of MI and reason for prescribed medications. 2. Begin instruction in activity program prescribed by physician.

Nursing Diagnosis: Knowledge Deficit Related to Noncompliance with Activity Program

Nursing Diagnosis Addressed	Knowledge deficit related to noncompliance with activity program
Teaching Directed To	Patient and significant other
Learning Enhancements/ Barriers	Patient is not experiencing any pain now and tends to overdo (B).
Method of Teaching	L, P, M, C (see Exhibit 10-1 for codes)
Instruction	1. Instructed in prescribed activity plan. "Activity Plan" handout left with patient and wife.

     2. Instructed in pathophysiology of MI: need for healing time and prescribed medications. Location of MI charted on a diagram.

Evaluation of Learning

Wife and patient both expressed the unreality of the situation. Patient feels activity program is too regimented.

Plan

1. Provide wife and patient with a contact person from community support group.
2. Bring American Heart Association film on activity program next visit.

Instruction

1. Instructed patient's wife in guidelines for sexual activity (see attached handout).
2. Patient and wife previewed film.
3. Instructed in complications secondary to noncompliance with medication regimen.

Evaluation of Learning

Patient and wife had several questions concerning activity plan. Wife asked questions pertaining to sexual activity when patient out of room. Stated he was very sensitive about the subject and she didn't want to upset him. Patient signed a contract to adhere to medication regimen.

Plan

1. Obtain film on "Sexual Activity after an MI" if available.
2. Contact one of his close friends who experienced an MI a year ago to talk with him if appropriate.
3. Contact physician for possible medical social worker referral.
4. Continue to follow patient 1 × week for further instruction and observation.

NOTES

1. R. McCorckle, and B. Gemino, "What Nurses Need to Know about Home Care," *Oncology Nursing Forum* 11, no. 6 (November/December 1984):63–69.
2. W. Phipps, B. Long, and N. Woods, eds., *Medical-Surgical Nursing: Concepts and Clinical Practice* (St. Louis: C. V. Mosby Co., 1987).
3. Ibid.
4. J. Luckmann, and K. Sorensen, *Medical-Surgical Nursing: A Psychophysiologic Approach*, 2nd ed. (Philadelphia: W.B. Saunders Co., 1980).
5. Ibid.

BIBLIOGRAPHY

Birmingham, J. *Home Care Planning Based on DRGs*. Bethany, Conn.: Fleschner Publishing Co., Philadelphia: J.B. Lippincott Co., 1986.

Cahill, M., ed. *Patient Teaching*. Springhouse, Penn.: Springhouse Corp., 1987.

Carpenito, L. *Nursing Diagnosis: Application to Clinical Practice*. Philadelphia: J.B. Lippincott Co., 1983.

Ciranowicz, M., Furan, C., Kupnick, S., Weiner, S., and Welsh, N., eds. *Patient Teaching Manual 1*. Springhouse, Penn.: Springhouse Corp., 1987.

Crist, J. "Teaching Time: The MI Client's Readiness to Learn." *Home Healthcare Nurse* 3, no. 5, (May-June 1985):56.

Crowther, M. "Sex Questions a Cardiac Patient May Be Too Scared to Ask." *RN* 10, no. 49 (November 1986):44–46.

Doenges, M. *Nursing Care Plans: Nursing Diagnosis in Planning Patient Care*. Philadelphia: F.A. Davis Co., 1984.

Fletcher, V. "An Individualized Teaching Program Following Primary Uncomplicated Myocardial Infarction." *Journal of Advanced Nursing* 2, no. 12 (March 1987):195–200.

Gould, J.E., and Wargo, J. *Home Health Nursing Care Plans*. Rockville, Md.: Aspen Publishers, Inc., 1987.

Jaffe, M., and Skidmore-Roth, L. *Medical-Surgical Nursing Care Plans*. Norwalk, Conn.: Appleton-Century-Crofts, 1986.

Liddy, K.G., and Crowley, C. "Do MI Patients Have the Information They Need for the Recovery Phase at Home?" *Home Healthcare Nurse* 3, no. 5 (May-June 1987):19–25.

Luckmann, J., and Sorensen, K. *Medical Surgical Nursing: A Psychophysiologic Approach*, 2nd ed. Philadelphia: W.B. Saunders Co., 1980.

McHatton, M. "A Theory for Timely Teaching." *American Journal of Nursing* 7, no. 85 (July 1985):798–800.

Moynihan, M. "Assessing the Educational Needs of Post–Myocardial Infarction Patients." *Nursing Clinics of North America* 3, no. 19 (September 1984):441–447.

Neal, M., et al. *Nursing Care Planning Guides for Long-Term Care*. Monterey, Calif.: Wadsworth Health Sciences & Pacific Palisades, Calif.: NURSECO, Inc., 1981.

Niskala, H. "The Role of Community Health Nurses in Cardiac Rehabilitation." *Home Healthcare Nurse* 3, no. 5 (May/June 1987):15–15.

Phipps, W., Long, B., and Woods, N., eds. *Medical-Surgical Nursing: Concepts and Clinical Practice*. St. Louis: C.V. Mosby Co., 1987.

Raleigh, E.H., and Odtohan, B.C. "The Effect of a Cardiac Teaching Program on Patient Rehabilitation." *Heart & Lung* 3, no. 16 (May 1987):311–317.

Thompson, J., McFarland, G., Hirsch, J., Tucker, S., and Bowers, A. *Clinical Nursing*. St. Louis: C.V. Mosby Co., 1986.

Ulrich, S., Canale, S., and Wendell, S. *Nursing Care Planning Guides: A Nursing Diagnosis Approach*. Philadelphia: W.B. Saunders Co., 1986.

Chapter 11

The Patient with Acquired Immune Deficiency Syndrome

Objectives

- To discuss briefly statistics, pathophysiology and signs and symptoms of acquired immune deficiency syndrome.
- To describe the assessment data needed to teach the patient with acquired immune deficiency syndrome.
- To identify nursing diagnoses related to the teaching needs of a patient with acquired immune deficiency syndrome.
- To provide a sample teaching plan for a patient with acquired immune deficiency syndrome including nursing diagnosis, learning objective, plan, and teaching methods.
- To provide a sample documentation guide for a patient with acquired immune deficiency syndrome addressing the nursing diagnoses identified in the teaching plan.

11

THE CONDITION

Acquired immune deficiency syndrome (AIDS) has become the health challenge of this decade. More than 30,000 adults in the United States are diagnosed with AIDS, not counting the number of unknown cases. There are more than 400 children with AIDS. It has been estimated that by the year 2000 there will be one million cases of AIDS in this country. The mortality rate approaches 100 percent.

The following groups in the population are at risk in the following order:

1. homosexual and bisexual men
2. IV drug abusers
3. hemophiliacs
4. heterosexuals
5. transfusion recipients.

AIDS is an infectious disease transmitted via contact with body fluids, blood, or blood products. Other modes of transmission are not known at this time. It is characterized by dysfunction of cell-mediated immunity. The HIV-1 and HIV-2 virus invade the host cells and cause a defect in cellular immunity that consists of a reversal of the usual ratio of T-helper cells to T-suppressor cells. T-helper cells are thought to assist in antibody formation, while the T-suppressor cells decrease the T-helper cells' activity. T-helper cells are usually present in a 2:1 ratio over T-suppressor cells. When the reversal occurs, the T-suppressor mechanisms dominate. This defect in cellular immunity results in significant immunologic abnormalities manifested clinically as the development of recurrent, often severe, infection and unusual malignancies.[1-3]

Clinical manifestations vary from patient to patient. Kaposi's sarcoma, a malignant tumor of the endothelium, and *Pneumocystis carinii* pneumonia are commonly seen. Other manifestations include fatigue, malaise, persistent weight loss, lymphadenopathy, fevers, arthralgias, and persistent diarrhea.

ASSESSMENT OF TEACHING NEEDS RELATED TO THE CONDITION

With the increasing number of AIDS victims, the nurse will be seeing more and more of these patients return to their homes for care. In the home, the nurse plays a vital role in educating all caregivers. The teaching must include symptom control, medication regimen, comfort measures, and protection measures.[4] In providing this teaching, the nurse must thoroughly assess the teaching needs of the patient and significant other.

When assessing the patient, recall the three areas to assess: education needs, learner readiness, and available resources. The patient's knowledge of his illness and care is multifaceted. Does the patient understand the normal immune response and how the AIDS virus affects it? Does he know measures to take to prevent the transmission of the virus? Can he recognize signs and symptoms of opportunistic infections and how to protect himself from such infections? Knowledge in these areas is vital to protection of the patient and those caring for him.

The patient should be assessed for knowledge regarding his medical regimen, including medications, diet, and activity. Both the patient and the caregiver need to be aware of precautions to take in providing a safe environment in the home for all involved. These include

- respiratory safeguards
- handling of secretions
- laundering guidelines
- housecleaning measures

- cleaning of kitchen and utensils
- involvement with pets
- sexual practices
- use of drugs.[5]

The patient should also be assessed for knowledge concerning the need for psychological support and the recognition of outside support and resources.

Learner readiness of the patient and significant other is vital not only to their teaching but to their survival. Due to the severity and terminal state of the disease, the patient and caregiver should be ready to learn before being discharged to home. But still, it is an area that should be assessed in the home. The patient's physical condition may be so deteriorated that he is unable to learn. The role of caregiver can be a very demanding and tiring job. The caregivers should be assessed carefully for their physical and mental readiness to provide care to the patient. Acceptance of the condition by both can be a factor that affects learner readiness.

Last, the available resources must be assessed. The abilities, both mental and physical, of the patient and the caregiver should be assessed. Do they have an internal support system, and are they aware of AIDS support groups, which many communities are now organizing? Another resource that should be considered is the nurse's ability to provide the necessary patient teaching. The treatment of AIDS in the home is a situation with which not all nurses have had experience. The nurse must not only be willing to care for and teach the patient but be up to date on the latest information concerning the care, treatment, and preventive measures to be taken when caring for him in the home.

NURSING DIAGNOSES RELATED TO TEACHING NEEDS

The nurse should formulate a nursing diagnosis or diagnoses after assessing the patient's teaching needs. The diagnostic category of knowledge deficit would be chosen from the approved diagnostic categories (see Appendix B). In choosing the category, the nurse confirms an actual need for knowledge and/or instruction. The latter part of the diagnosis should identify areas of needed instruction (see Exhibit 2-1).

After assessing the patient, the nurse may consider any of the following as areas in which a knowledge deficit may exist:

- disease process
- transmission of disease and prevention of transmission
- measures to prevent infections
- medical regimen
- safety precautions to be taken in the home
- community resources.

The following are examples of possible nursing diagnoses:

- knowledge deficit related to the disease process
- knowledge deficit related to the prevention of infections
- knowledge deficit related to transmission of the AIDS virus
- knowledge deficit related to home management
- knowledge deficit related to community resources.

For the purpose of this discussion, three nursing diagnoses are identified. When developing a plan for an actual patient, the number of diagnoses will vary depending on the condition and needs of the patient and significant other. From these diagnoses, the nurse formulates a teaching plan and patient goals. See Appendix C for guides assisting the nurse in assessing the patient's teaching needs, developing a teaching plan, and documenting the plan after implementation.

SAMPLE TEACHING PLAN

A sample teaching plan for AIDS patients is shown in Exhibit 11-1.

SAMPLE DOCUMENTATION GUIDES

Nursing Diagnosis: Knowledge Deficit Related to the Prevention of Infection

Nursing Diagnosis Addressed	Knowledge deficit related to the prevention of infection
Teaching Directed To	Patient and significant other

Learning Enhancements/ Barriers	1. Patient in denial phase (B) 2. Patient concerned significant other will leave him (B) (verbalized by significant other) 3. Significant other very supportive (E)
Method of Teaching	L, G, P (see Exhibit 11-1 for codes)

Instruction	1. Instructed in common illnesses of AIDS:
	  • *Pneumocystis carinii*
	  • pneumonia (PCP)
	  • cytomegalovirus (CMV)
	  • herpes etc., due to depressed immune system.
	2. Instructed in "Guidelines to Prevent Infection." See teaching plan for specific list. Handout given to patient and significant other.
	3. Instructed significant other that he was probably more of a risk to the patient than the patient was to him due to spread of infections. Instructed in signs and symptoms of infection.

Evaluation of Learning	Patient appeared indifferent at times during instruction. Significant other appeared interested and comprehended. Significant other stated: "He just hasn't accepted the diagnosis yet."
Plan	1. Obtain physician order for medical social worker referral. 2. Provide them with 800 number for AIDS information hotline. 3. Provide resource material each visit. 4. Assess comprehension of instruction next visit.

Note: (B) Barriers
    (E) Enhancements

Exhibit 11-1 Sample Teaching Plan: AIDS

Patient's Name _____

Nursing Diagnosis	Learning Objective	Plan	Teaching Method*	Date Plan Established	Initials
Knowledge deficit related to the prevention of infection	The patient will identify three ways to decrease the risk of infection.	Instruct in: 1. Guidelines to prevent infection: a. avoid crowds and people with known infections b. adequate rest c. maintain nutrition d. practice good hygiene e. avoid foreign travel. 2. Identify signs and symptoms that indicate the presence of infection: a. fever b. chills c. swollen glands d. night sweats.	1. L, G, P 2. L, P	3/18/87	E. J., R.N.

Knowledge deficit related to the transmission of the AIDS virus	Identify three ways to prevent the spread of AIDS.	Instruct in ways to prevent the spread of AIDS: 1. handwashing 2. cover mouth when coughing or sneezing 3. practice safe sex 4. do not donate blood.	L, G, D, P, C, M	3/18/87 · E. J., R.N.
Knowledge deficit related to home management	Identify eight areas of precaution to be considered in home care.	Instruct in the following guidelines for home care: 1. respiratory safeguards 2. treatment precautions 3. laundry techniques 4. housecleaning 5. kitchen care 6. pets 7. sex 8. drugs.	1. L, G, P, M 2. L, P, M 3. L, D, R, P 4. L, D, R, P 5. L, D, R, P 6. L, D, R, P 7. L, P, C, G 8. L, G, P, C, M	3/31/87 · E. J., R.N.

*Method of teaching codes: L = lecture; G = group discussion; D = demonstration; R = role playing; P = programmed instruction; C = contracts; M = media.

**Nursing Diagnosis: Knowledge Deficit Related to the
  Transmission of the AIDS Virus**

Nursing Diagnosis Addressed	Knowledge deficit related to the transmission of the AIDS virus
Teaching Directed To	Patient and significant other
Learning Enhancements/ Barriers	1. Patient in denial phase (B) 2. Patient concerned significant other will leave him (B) (verbalized by significant other) 3. Significant other very supportive (E)
Method of Teaching	L, P (see Exhibit 11-1 for codes)
Instruction	1. Instructed in "Ways to Prevent the Spread of AIDS." Handout and literature left with patient and significant other.
Evaluation of Learning	1. Patient would not come into room during instruction. Directed to significant other. 2. Significant other was able to identify three ways to decrease infection and signs and symptoms of infection.
Plan	1. Significant other will instruct patient in this initial phase of denial. 2. R.N. will continue to develop a trusting relationship with patient. 3. Will seek support group for patient and significant other. None available in small community they live in.

Nursing Diagnosis: Knowledge Deficit Related to Home Management

Nursing Diagnosis Addressed	Knowledge deficit related to home management
Teaching Directed To	Patient and significant other
Learning Enhancements/ Barriers	1. Patient in denial phase (B) 2. Patient concerned significant other will leave him (B) (verbalized by significant other) 3. Significant other very supportive (E)
Method of Teaching	L, P (see Exhibit 11-1 for codes)
Instruction	Instructed in respiratory safeguards and treatment precautions. Written instructions left with significant other.
Evaluation of Learning	1. Patient more receptive today; listened to instructions. 2. Able to identify ways to prevent spread of AIDS.
Plan	Instruct in home cleaning techniques next visit.
Teaching Directed To	Patient and significant other
Learning Enhancements/ Barriers	Patient more accepting of diagnosis for time being (E)
Method of Teaching	L, P, D, M (see Exhibit 11-1 for codes)
Instruction	1. Instructed in laundry techniques: linen that has been contaminated by body

fluids should be washed separately and with a disinfectant.

2. The Centers for Disease Control recommends using [29]sodium hypochloride to clean contaminated floors, beds, etc.[6]
3. Proper dishwashing techniques should be used; dishwasher if possible.
4. Demonstrated proper techniques for handling soiled laundry.
5. Handwritten precautions and guidelines given to significant other. List of suitable disinfectants also left with significant other.

Evaluation of Learning

Patient and significant other appeared to understand and comprehend instructions; asked several questions.

Plan

1. Bring film on "Safe Sex" next visit.
2. Evaluate comprehension of previous instructions.
3. Medical social worker to visit tomorrow for financial planning, counseling, and support.
3. Will decrease visits to 1 × week next visit if teaching has been comprehended. Teaching will continue and plan revised as patient needs change.

Teaching Directed To

Patient and significant other

Method of Teaching

L, P, M (see Exhibit 11-1 for codes)

Instruction

Film "Safe Sex" previewed by patient and significant other.

Evaluation of Learning

1. Patient and significant other had few questions. Appeared to be embarrassed to discuss with R.N.

	2. Evaluated comprehension of teaching previously instructed: comprehension good.
Plan	Check with medical social worker for follow up on sexual safety teaching.
Teaching Directed To	Patient and significant other
Method of Teaching	L, P (see Exhibit 11-1 for codes)
Instruction	Instructed in drug precautions. Literature and written precautions left with patient and significant other.
Evaluation of Learning	Patient and significant other appeared to comprehend.
Plan	Decrease skilled R.N. visits to 1 × week.

NOTES

1. S. Ulrich, S. Canale, and S. Wendell, *Nursing Care Planning Guides: A Nursing Diagnosis Approach* (Philadelphia: W.B. Saunders Co., 1986).

2. J. Thompson, G. McFarland, J. Hirsch, S. Tucker, and A. Bowers, *Clinical Nursing* (St. Louis: C.V. Mosby Co., 1986).

3. E. Garvey, "Guidelines for Caring for the AIDS Patient in the Home Setting," *National Intravenous Therapy Association* 8 (1985):481–483.

4. J. Martin, "Challenges in Caring for the Person with AIDS at Home," *Caring*, June 1986, pp. 12–20.

5. K. Dhundale and P. Hubbard, "Home Care for the AIDS Patient: Safety First," *Nursing* 16, no. 9 (September 1986):34–36.

6. M. Neighbors, "Care of the Home Health AIDS Victim," *Home Health Journal* 8, no. 8 (August 1987).

BIBLIOGRAPHY

Bennett, J.A. "HTLV-III AIDS Link." *American Journal of Nursing* 85, no. 10 (October 1987).

Birmingham, J. *Home Care Planning Based on DRGs*. Bethany, Conn.: Fleschner Publishing Co., Philadelphia: J.B. Lippincott Co., 1986.

Broshan, S. "Our First Home Care AIDS Patient: Maria." *Nursing* 9, no. 16 (September 1986): 37–39.

Bryant, J.K. "Home Care of the Client with AIDS." *Journal of Community Health Nursing* 2, no. 3 (1986):69–74.

Cahill, M., ed. *Patient Teaching*. Springhouse, Penn.: Springhouse Corp., 1987.

Carpenito, L. *Nursing Diagnosis: Application to Clinical Practice*. Philadelphia: J.B. Lippincott Co., 1983.

Ciranowicz, M., Furan, C., Kupnick, S., Weiner, S., and Welsh, N., eds. *Patient Teaching Manual 1*. Springhouse, Penn.: Springhouse Corp., 1987.

Dhundale, K., and Hubbard, P. "Home Care for the AIDS Patient: Safety First." *Nursing* 16, no. 9 (September 1986):34–36.

Doenges, M. *Nursing Care Plans: Nursing Diagnosis in Planning Patient Care*. Philadelphia: F.A. Davis Co., 1984.

Garvey, E. "Guidelines for Caring for the AIDS Patient in the Home Setting." *National Intravenous Therapy Association* 8 (1985):481–583.

Gould, J.E., and Wargo, J. *Home Health Nursing Care Plans*. Rockville, Md.: Aspen Publishers, Inc., 1987.

Horne, E.M. "AIDS: Informing Patients and Clients." *Professional Nurse* 5, no. 2 (February 1987):144–146.

Hughes, M.M. "Aftercare Instruction: AIDS Brochure." *Journal of Emergency Nursing* 6, no. 9 (November/December 1983):340–342.

Jaffe, M., and Skidmore-Roth, L. *Medical-Surgical Nursing Care Plans*. Norwalk, Conn.: Appleton-Century-Crofts, 1986.

Kaplan, H.S., Sager, C.J., and Schiavi, R.C. "AIDS and the Sex Therapist." *Journal of Sexuality and Marital Therapy* 4, no. 11 (Winter 1985):210–214.

Krapfl, M. "As AIDS Hysteria Spreads, So Does Need for Cool-Headed Education." *Occupational Health Staffing* 4, no. 55 (April 1986):20–29.

Luckmann, J., and Sorensen, K. *Medical Surgical Nursing: A Psychophysiologic Approach*, 2nd ed. Philadelphia: W.B. Saunders Co., 1980.

Martin, J. "Challenges in Caring for the Person with AIDS at Home." *Caring*, June 1986, pp. 12–20.

McCormick, B. "AIDS Leads to New Education Products Market." *Hospitals* 18, no. 60 (September 1986):87–88.

Mills, M., Woofsy, C.B., and Mills, J. "The Acquired Immunodeficiency Syndrome: Infection Control and Public Health Law." *New England Journal of Medicine* 14 (1987):931–936.

Neal, M., Cohen, P., and Cooper, P. *Nursing Care Planning Guides for Long-Term Care*. Monterey, Calif.: Wadsworth Health Sciences & Pacific Palisades, Calif.: NURSECO, Inc., 1981.

Neighbors, M. "Care of the Home Health AIDS Victims." *Home Health Journal* 8, no. 8 (1987).

Perdew, S. "AIDS and Infection Control." *Caring*, June 1986, pp. 22–26.

Phipps, W., Long, B., and Woods, N., eds. *Medical-Surgical Nursing: Concepts and Clinical Practice*. St. Louis: C.V. Mosby Co., 1987.

Porter, S. "What to Tell Your Patients about AIDS." *Ohio Medicine* 4, no. 83 (April 1987): 262–263.

Thompson, J., McFarland, G., Hirsch, J., Tucker, S., and Bowers, A. *Clinical Nursing*. St. Louis: C.V. Mosby Co., 1986.

Ulrich, S., Canale, S., and Wendell, S. *Nursing Care Planning Guides: A Nursing Diagnosis Approach*. Philadelphia: W.B. Saunders Co., 1986.

Ungvarski, P. "Learning to Live with AIDS." *Nursing Mirror* 21, no. 160 (May 1985):20–22.

Chapter 12

The Patient Receiving Parenteral Medications

Objectives

- To discuss briefly statistics, pathophysiology and signs and symptoms of parenteral medicine.
- To describe the assessment data needed to teach the patient with parenteral medicine.
- To identify nursing diagnoses related to the teaching needs of a patient with parenteral medicine.
- To provide a sample teaching plan for a patient with parenteral medicine including nursing diagnosis, learning objective, plan, and teaching methods.
- To provide a sample documentation guide for a patient with parenteral medicine addressing the nursing diagnoses identified in the teaching plan.

12

THE CONDITION

In the last ten years, home parenteral therapy has come from the administration of simple replacement fluids to the administration of complex nutritional solutions, antibiotics, and chemotherapy. These patients, if not able to go home, would have remained in the hospital for many days. "Through home care, they are allowed to maintain a more normal lifestyle and remain in a supportive and familiar environment with family and friends."[1]

There are many conditions that could warrant home parenteral therapy. Patients who are treated at home with IV antibiotics may have one of the following diseases:

- acute osteomyelitis
- acute bacterial endocarditis
- septic arthritis
- cystic fibrosis
- chronic urinary tract infections
- central nervous system infections.

The following are some types of cancer treated at home with chemotherapy:

- breast cancer
- Hodgkin's disease
- lung cancer
- Burkett's lymphoma
- acute and chronic lymphocytic leukemia
- ovarian cancer
- testicular cancer
- skin cancer.

The following are conditions the patient receiving home total parenteral nutrition may have:

- inflammatory bowel disease
- cancer
- children with birth defects
- surgical intervention of the digestive tract
- bowel obstruction
- short bowel syndrome.[2]

The lists are not inclusive. Caring for a patient receiving home parenteral therapy is a true challenge to the patient care team. The nurse becomes the primary person responsible for patient and caregiver education. She must have a sound knowledge base concerning parenteral therapy and be highly skillful in its techniques.

ASSESSMENT OF TEACHING NEEDS RELATED TO THE CONDITION

There are many areas of assessment the nurse should consider when assessing the patient receiving home parenteral therapy. This text's emphasis is on patient teaching; therefore, recall the areas to assess for patient teaching: educational needs, learner readiness, and the teaching situation. Through assessment of these areas, the teaching needs can be established.

The nurse is responsible for gathering information that determines if the patient and family are capable of handling the high-tech care of IV therapy in the home. Some programs have written into their policies guidelines that must be assessed:

- Does the patient understand the treatment program, inherent risks, and financial requirements?
- Is the patient motivated, and does he possess average mental capabilities?
- How do the patient's veins look? Are there several peripheral sites to choose from?
- Is there a family member or close friend who is willing to learn about the treatment also?
- Does the patient have a telephone and a freezer?
- Is there transportation available for emergency situations?[3]

All of these guidelines do not relate to establishing the patient's educational needs, but they do assist in screening the patient, which is one of two mechanisms identified in controlling failure rates. The other is the education of the patient and family.[4]

When assessing the patient and caregiver for teaching needs, the following questions must be asked:

- Do they understand the purpose of the therapy?
- Did they retain any of the skills taught while in the hospital?
- Does the patient understand aseptic technique?
- Can they demonstrate the required equipment and supplies?
- Do they possess knowledge about the prescribed drug?
- Do they know precautions to take?
- Can they demonstrate administration of the drug?

There are many details to be covered. The nurse must remember that the patient is being taught a skill at home that is usually performed by a professional in the hospital. The patient must learn about gravity, pumps, methods of operation, alarm systems, self-connection, self-infusion, self-disconnection, rates of administration, catheter care, monitoring vital signs, weights, blood glucose, or other parameters indicated for the safe administration of parenteral fluids in the home. The nurse can create problems in a controlled atmosphere and see how the patient and caregiver respond. Assessment of these areas will establish the patient's teaching needs.

The patient and caregiver must be highly motivated and enthusiastic. They must be physically and mentally capable of learning and performing these skills. Their readiness will depend greatly on the underlying condition. A patient who is receiving IV therapy for 6 weeks for bacterial endocarditis may be much more motivated than a patient who has a malignancy and will be receiving total parenteral nutrition for an indefinite time. Learner readiness must be present in establishing home parenteral therapy.

The teaching situation is a very important aspect to consider. The physical environment should be able to accommodate equipment and supplies. An area for patient teaching should be available and comfortable to the patient, as this therapy entails extensive teaching. As always, the person who chooses to assist as caregiver must be ready and willing to learn along with the patient. Resources must be assessed. Is there financial and social support? The patient and caregiver will also need to be made aware of professional and community resources available to them. The specifics of these will depend on the underlying condition. Through the assessment and establishment of teaching needs, these patients are free from lengthy hospital stays and allowed to lead a near normal life.

NURSING DIAGNOSES RELATED TO TEACHING NEEDS

After assessing the patient's teaching needs, the nurse can formulate a nursing diagnosis or diagnoses. The diagnostic category of knowledge deficit would be chosen from the 72 approved diagnostic categories (see Appendix B). In choosing this category, the nurse is confirming an actual need for knowledge and/or instruction. The latter part of the statement would indicate the area in which the patient needs instruction (see Exhibit 2-1).

When establishing a nursing diagnosis for the patient receiving parenteral medications, the following areas may be included:

• purpose of therapy
• medical regimen

- type of vascular access
- aseptic technique
- drug administration
- catheter care
- potential problems and how to handle them.

Examples of possible nursing diagnoses are

- knowledge deficit related to purpose of IV therapy
- knowledge deficit related to assembling solution and tubing
- knowledge deficit related to type of drug being administered
- knowledge deficit related to catheter care
- knowledge deficit related to signs and symptoms of phlebitis.

For the purpose of this discussion, three diagnoses are identified and a sample teaching care plan developed with examples of documentation for the plan. The actual patient may have one or many diagnoses. From these diagnoses, the nurse formulates a teaching plan with patient goals. See Appendix C for guides assisting the nurse in assessing the patient's teaching needs, developing a teaching plan, and documenting the plan after implementation.

SAMPLE TEACHING PLAN

A sample teaching plan for these patients is shown in Exhibit 12-1.

SAMPLE DOCUMENTATION GUIDES

Nursing Diagnosis: Knowledge Deficit Related to Purpose of IV Therapy

Nursing Diagnosis Addressed	Knowledge deficit related to purpose of IV therapy

Exhibit 12-1 Sample Teaching Plan: Parenteral Medication

Patient's Name

Nursing Diagnosis	Learning Objective	Plan	Teaching Method*	Date Plan Established	Initials
Knowledge deficit related to purpose of IV therapy	Identify why patient is receiving IV therapy.	Instruct in: 1. the purposes of IV therapy 2. the specifics concerning the therapy, i.e., the need for long-term antibiotic therapy.	1. L, P, M 2. L, D, R, P, C, M	3/11/87	E. J., R.N.
Knowledge deficit related to type of drug being administered	Verbalize name of drug, action, usual dosage, side effects, and rate of administration.	Instruct in the following: 1. Identify type of drug given. 2. Instruct patient in drug action, usual dosage, side effects, and rate of administration.	1. L, P 2. L, D, R, P, C, M	3/11/87	E. J., R.N.
Knowledge deficit related to catheter care	Demonstrate care of catheter.	Instruct in: 1. Identify type of catheter used. 2. Demonstrate care of catheter. 3. Provide written list with steps of catheter care.	1. L, D, M 2. L, D, R, M 3. L, D, P	3/11/87	E. J., R.N.

*Method of teaching codes: L = lecture; G = group discussion; D = demonstration; R = role playing; P = programmed instruction; C = contracts; M = media.

Teaching Directed To	Significant other

Learning Enhancements/ Barriers
1. Significant other supportive, intelligent, and willing to learn (E)
2. Patient too ill to comprehend instructions (B)

Method of Teaching L, P (see Exhibit 12-1 for codes)

Instruction Instructed significant other in purpose of IV antibiotic therapy, pathophysiology of disease process.

Evaluation of Learning Significant other attentive; appeared to comprehend instructions.

Plan Begin instructing significant other in basics of drug administration next visit.

Nursing Diagnosis: Knowledge Deficit Related to Type of Drug Being Administered

Nursing Diagnosis Addressed Knowledge deficit related to type of drug being administered

Teaching Directed To Significant other

Method of Teaching L, P (see Exhibit 12-1 for codes)

Instruction
1. Identified drug prescribed by physician. Proper handling of drug, refrigerate, etc. Handwritten instructions left with significant other.
2. Instructed in pertinent drugs, actions, side effects, dosage, etc. Left written instruction with significant other. (Doc-

Note: (B) Barriers
(E) Enhancements

	umentation of medications outlined in previous Documentation Guide. Specific prescribed drug should be instructed in as indicated.)
Evaluation of Learning	Significant other overwhelmed with the amount of information given.
Plan	1. Instruct in-depth during instruction of drug administration.

Nursing Diagnosis: Knowledge Deficit Related to Catheter Care

Nursing Diagnosis Addressed	Knowledge deficit related to catheter care
Teaching Directed To	Significant other
Learning Enhancements/ Barriers	Significant other very apprehensive concerning administration of drug (B)
Method of Teaching	L, P, D (see Exhibit 12-1 for codes)
Instruction	1. Patient has a subclavian line with Broviac catheter. 2. Drew location of catheter on diagram to emphasize importance of catheter care (see nurse's notes 3/10). 3. Demonstrated catheter care to significant other in a step-by-step fashion. 4. Left "Broviac Catheter Care" instructions with significant other to study.
Evaluation of Learning	Significant other very nervous and apprehensive about catheter care; afraid she will dislodge it.
Plan	1. Continue catheter care instructions until significant other is adept at procedure. 2. Allow significant other to glove next visit.

Teaching Directed To	Significant other
Learning Enhancements/ Barriers	Significant other determined to overcome fear (E)
Method of Teaching	L, P, D (see Exhibit 12-1 for codes)
Evaluation of Learning	Significant other accomplished proper gloving technique after several attempts. Feels more confident now. Asked several questions.
Plan	Allow significant other to remove bandage next visit under supervision.
Teaching Directed To	Significant other
Instruction	Instructed in proper removal of bandage, disposal of soiled bandages, and signs and symptoms to assess at catheter site when bandage is removed.
Evaluation of Learning	Significant other removed bandage without incident using proper technique and without contamination. This was accomplished very slowly and with close supervision.
Plan	Demonstrate cleansing of the site next dressing change.
Learning Enhancements/ Barriers	1. Significant other very receptive to teaching: overcoming apprehension (E)
Instruction	Instructed in disconnecting and connecting IV tubing of administration set. Written precautions given to significant other and instructed in same.

Evaluation of Learning	Significant other appeared to comprehend.
Plan	Assess comprehension at next visit. Allow significant other to change IV solution administration sets.

Nursing Diagnosis: Knowledge Deficit Related to Catheter Care

Nursing Diagnosis Addressed	Knowledge deficit related to catheter care
Teaching Directed To	Significant other
Instruction	Instructed and demonstrated proper cleansing method using aseptic technique. Written instructions given to patient and instructed in same.
Evaluation of Learning	1. Significant other removed bandage without incident; watched procedure attentively. 2. Significant other hung PM dosage with close supervision and step-by-step instruction. Had difficulty trying to handle tubing without contaminating.
Plan	Allow significant other to hang AM dosage and do PM dressing change.
Nursing Diagnosis Addressed 3/13 AM Visit	Same as 3/12
Teaching Directed To	Significant other
Learning Enhancements/ Barriers	Same as 3/12

Method of Teaching	L, P, D (see Exhibit 12-1 for codes)
Instruction	Instructed in dressing change. Written instruction sheet left with significant other. Cautioned significant other concerning aseptic technique.
Evaluation of Learning	Allowed significant other to do complete dressing change. Had to reglove × 2 due to contamination but otherwise did very well. Conscientious about technique. Was able to change dressing, IV tubing, and administration set without incident.
Plan	Allow significant other to do complete dressing change.
Nursing Diagnosis Addressed 3/13 PM Visit	Same as 3/12
Teaching Directed To	Significant other
Learning Enhancements/ Barriers	Same as 3/12
Method of Teaching	L, P, D (see Exhibit 12-1 for codes)
Instruction	Instructed in dressing change from start to finish.
Evaluation of Learning	1. Significant other verbalized and demonstrated dressing change on doll. 2. Allowed significant other to do complete dressing change. Had to reglove × 2 due to contamination but otherwise did very well. Was able to change dressing, IV tubing, and administration set without incident.

Plan	Observe dressing change at PM visit tomorrow; if technique satisfactory, will decrease visits to 1 × day for observation and continued teaching.
Nursing Diagnosis Addressed 3/14 AM Visit	Same as 3/12
Teaching Directed To	Significant other
Learning Enhancements/ Barriers	Same as 3/12
Method of Teaching	L, D (see Exhibit 12-1 for codes)
Instruction	Instructed in aseptic techniques to remember.
Evaluation of Learning	Significant other hung AM dosage without breaking aseptic technique.
Plan	Observe dressing change at PM visit.
Nursing Diagnosis Addressed 3/14 PM Visit	Same as 3/12
Teaching Directed To	Significant other
Learning Enhancements/ Barriers	Same as 3/12
Method of Teaching	L, D (see Exhibit 12-1 for codes)
Instruction	Allowed significant other to identify areas in dressing change she felt uncomfortable with. Instructed in those areas; cleansing

around catheter, applying antibiotic oint-
ment to dressing without contaminating
dressing, etc.

Plan   Significant other accomplished dressing
change without breaking aseptic technique. Will decrease visits to 1 × day. PM
visit to observe dressing changes × 2 or 3
more days, then reduce visits as indicated.

NOTES

1. P. Smith, "Quality Standards in High-Tech I.V. Home Care," *Caring*, September 1986, p. 91.

2. C. Gardner, "Home I.V. Therapy: Part I," *National Intravenous Therapy Association* 9 (1986): 95–103.

3. Ibid.

4. R. Bergers, J. Martin, and B. Streckfus, "A Home I.V. Antibiotic Program," *National Intravenous Therapy Association* 8 (1985):238–239.

BIBLIOGRAPHY

Ford, R.D., ed. *MediQuick* (Springhouse, Penn.: Springhouse Corp., 1987), p. 88.

Gardner, C. "Home I.V. Therapy: Part I." *National Intravenous Therapy Association* 9 (1986): 95–103.

Gardner, C. "Home I.V. Therapy: Part II." *National Intravenous Therapy Association* 9 (1986): 193–203.

Garvey, E.C. "Current and Future Nursing Issues in the Home Administration of Chemotherapy." *Seminar in Oncology Nursing* 2, no. 3 (May 1987):142–147.

Holmes, W. "SQ Chemotherapy at Home." *American Journal of Nursing* 85, no. 2 (February 1985):168–169.

Jaffe, M., and Skidmore-Roth, L. *Medical-Surgical Nursing Care Plans*. Norwalk, Conn.: Appleton-Century-Crofts, 1986.

Kasmer, R.J., Horsington, L.M., and Yukniewicz, S. "Home Parenteral Antibiotic Therapy, Part I: An Overview of Program Design." *Home Health Care Nurse* 5, no. 1 (1987):12–18.

Kinstantinides, N.N. "Home Parenteral Nutrition: A Viable Alternative for Patients with Cancer." *Oncology Nurse Forum* 1, no. 12 (January/February 1985):23–29.

Koithan, M. "Home Total Parenteral Nutrition Complications." *National Intravenous Therapy Association* 8 (1985):231–237.

"Learning to Care for Your Hickman/Broviac Catheter." *Oncology Nurse Forum* 4, no. 9 (February 1982):61–62.

Luckmann, J., and Sorensen, K. *Basic Nursing: A Psychophysiologic Approach*, 2nd ed. Philadelphia: W.B. Saunders Co., 1986.

Luckmann, J., and Sorensen, K. *Medical Surgical Nursing: A Psychophysiologic Approach*, 2nd ed. Philadelphia: W.B. Saunders Co., 1980.

May, C. "Antibiotic Therapy at Home." *American Journal of Nursing* 84, no. 3 (March 1984): 348–349.

Neal, M., Cohen, P., and Cooper, P. *Nursing Care Planning Guides for Long-Term Care.* Monterey, Calif.: Wadsworth Health Sciences & Pacific Palisades, Calif.: NURSECO, Inc., 1981.

Padilla, G.V., and Grant, M.M. "Psychosocial Aspects of Artificial Feeding." *Cancer* (Suppl. 1) (January 1985):301–304.

Phipps, W., Long, B., and Woods, N., eds. *Medical-Surgical Nursing: Concepts and Clinical Practice.* St. Louis: C.V. Mosby Co., 1987.

Pozzi, M., and Peck, N. "An Option for the Patient with Chronic Osteomyelitis: Home Intravenous Antibiotic Therapy." *Orthopedic Nursing* 5, no. 5 (September/October 1986): 9–14, 54.

Schad, R.F., and Lucaroti, R.L. "Patient Teaching Program for Home Intravenous Antimicrobial Therapy." *American Journal Hospital Pharmacology*, 2, no. 43 (February 1986): 372–375.

Smith, P. "Quality Standards in High-Tech I.V. Home Care." *Caring*, September 1986, pp. 90–94.

Swenson, J.P. "Training Patients to Administer Intravenous Antibiotics at Home." *American Journal of Hospital Pharmacy* 10, no. 38 (December 1981):1480–1483.

Teich, C.J., and Raia, K. "Teaching Strategies for an Ambulatory Chemotherapy Program." *Oncology Nurse Forum* 5, no. 11 (September/October 1984):24–28.

Thompson, J., McFarland, G., Hirsch, J., Tucker, S., and Bowers, A. *Clinical Nursing.* St. Louis: C.V. Mosby Co., 1986.

Thomson, S., and Lang, K. "The I.V. Solution: A Home Care Alternative." *National Intravenous Therapy Association* 5 (1984):397–400.

Ulrich, S., Canale, S., and Wendell, S. *Nursing Care Planning Guides: A Nursing Diagnosis Approach.* Philadelphia: W.B. Saunders Co., 1986.

Wiseman, M. "Setting Standards for Home I.V. Therapy." *American Journal of Nursing* 85, no. 4 (April 1985):421–422.

Chapter 13

The Patient Who Needs Mechanical Ventilation

Objectives

- To discuss briefly statistics, pathophysiology and signs and symptoms of the ventilator-dependent patient.
- To describe the assessment data needed to teach the ventilator-dependent patient.
- To identify nursing diagnoses related to the teaching needs of the ventilator-dependent patient.
- To provide a sample teaching plan for the ventilator-dependent patient including nursing diagnosis, learning objective, plan, and teaching methods.
- To provide a sample documentation guide for the ventilator-dependent patient addressing the nursing diagnoses identified in the teaching plan.

13

THE CONDITION

Mechanical ventilation is indicated for patients who are unable to maintain adequate ventilation on their own. Before 1981, this patient was hospitalized for as long as ventilatory assistance was necessary. In 1981, a young child who was ventilatory-dependent was allowed to go home and be cared for by her family. The concept of home ventilation became a reality.[1] "At least 3,000 ventilator-dependent patients are being successfully cared for at home."[2] Although this is a small percentage of the number of ventilator-dependent patients, it is a great stride toward providing high-tech care in the home. For the patients who can be cared for at home, there is greater cost-effectiveness and improved quality of life.

Patients who are able to return home are classified into three categories. In the first group are patients who are unable to maintain spontaneous ventilatory function over prolonged periods. They usually have neuromuscular and thoracic wall disorders such as multiple sclerosis, myasthenia gravis, diaphragmatic paralysis, and amyotrophic lateral sclerosis. The second group have ventilatory failure associated with long-term survival and are stable but still require continuous mechanical ventilation. They include those with high spinal cord injuries, late-stage

189

muscular dystrophy, apneic encephalopathies, and severe chronic obstructive lung disease. The third group are terminally ill and have stable ventilatory failure; their life expectancy is short. The diseases involved are lung cancer and end-stage chronic obstructive lung disease.[3]

There are many advantages for the mechanically ventilated patient to be cared for in his home and few disadvantages:

Advantages

- Positive impact on the patient and family
- Allows patient to participate in decision making processes
- Participation in the family's daily activities
- More normal routine
- Increased independence
- Improved morale for patient and family
- Increased willingness to participate in the prescribed regimen
- Increased mobility
- Decreased risk of nosocomial infections
- Improved nutritional status
- Decreased cost.

Disadvantages

- Increase burden on family
- Lack of outside support systems
- Increase electrical demand in home
- Potential equipment malfunction
- Reimbursement for nursing care.[4]

Through the proper selection of patients for home ventilation, many of the complications that occur can be avoided. All cases should be viewed individually. To be successful, a thorough and organized assessment of the patient and caregiver must be completed, including the assessment of teaching needs.

ASSESSMENT OF TEACHING NEEDS RELATED TO THE CONDITION

The literature clearly points out the advantages to the mechanical ventilator-dependent patient returning home. The teaching needs required to maintain such a patient in the home are great. Usually, patients are allowed a 48-hour trial period at home to see how they and other caregivers function. Obviously, a great deal of patient teaching must be done in the hospital, but upon returning home, the patient and his caregiver will need frequent guidance and instruction.

In assessing the patient and caregiver for their educational needs, recall the areas to assess: educational need, learner readiness, and the teaching situation. When assessing the educational needs, much of what the nurse does will be observing the patient and caregiver demonstrate the techniques and skills they have learned, such as airway assessment, bagging technique, sterile suctioning, tracheostomy (trach) care, care of the ventilator, and troubleshooting problems.[5] Other areas to assess include the caregiver's mental and physical ability to deal with the rigorous daily schedule, including cleaning equipment, suctioning, and recognizing the signs and symptoms of respiratory infections and other nonrespiratory complications. Do they know how to handle life-threatening situations such as trach tube dislodgement or a power failure?

The patient and the caregiver must be emotionally, mentally, and physically ready to learn the skills necessary to provide the care needed. Other physical problems may delay the patient's readiness to learn. The patient and caregiver who appeared very capable in the hospital may be overwhelmed in the home. Usually, these patients and caregivers need a great deal of support and instruction.

The teaching situation should be one in which the patient and caregiver feel comfortable in demonstrating their new skills and asking questions when in doubt. Another area that must be addressed is the ability of the nurse to teach the ventilator-dependent patient. If a nurse has not worked in a critical care area, it is likely she has never worked with a ventilator. Before taking on such a patient, the nurse should gain the knowledge and skills necessary to care for such a patient in the home setting. Home health agencies who anticipate admitting ventilator-dependent patients should contract with a respiratory therapist to ensure quality care for these patients.

Through a thorough assessment of teaching needs and the provision of the necessary education, the experience of caring for the ventilator-dependent patient can be highly rewarding for both the patient and caregiver.

NURSING DIAGNOSES RELATED TO TEACHING NEEDS

With the assessment completed, the nurse can formulate a nursing diagnosis or diagnoses. The diagnostic category of knowledge deficit would be chosen from the 72 approved diagnostic categories (see Appendix B). In choosing this category, the nurse is confirming an actual need for knowledge and/or instruction. The latter part of the statement indicates the area in which the patient needs instruction (see Exhibit 2-1).

When considering the ventilator-dependent patient and his caregiver, the following areas may be included:

- medical regimen
- airway assessment
- techniques related to ventilator care
- signs and symptoms of complications
- available resources.

Examples of possible diagnoses are

- knowledge deficit related to airway assessment
- knowledge deficit related to sterile suctioning
- knowledge deficit related to recognizing respiratory infection
- knowledge deficit related to actions to be taken if patient has obstructed airway.

For the purpose of this discussion, three diagnoses are identified and a sample teaching care plan developed with examples of documentation for the plan. The actual patient may have one or several diagnoses. From these diagnoses, the nurse formulates the teaching plan, including patient goals. See Appendix C for guides assisting the nurse in assessing the patient's teaching needs, developing a teaching plan, and documenting the plan after implementation.

SAMPLE TEACHING PLAN

A sample teaching plan for these patients is shown in Exhibit 13-1.

SAMPLE DOCUMENTATION GUIDES

Nursing Diagnosis: Knowledge Deficit Related to Sterile Suctioning

Nursing Diagnosis Addressed	Knowledge deficit related to sterile suctioning
Teaching Directed To	Significant other (wife)
Learning Enhancements/ Barriers	1. Patient too ill to comprehend instructions (B) 2. Significant other slow learner (B) 3. Significant other willing and eager to learn (E)
Method of Teaching	L, P, D (see Exhibit 13-1 for codes)
Instruction	1. Instructed significant other in rationale for sterile technique and appropriate equipment. 2. Written instruction sheet left: "Proper Suctioning Technique." 3. Demonstrated suctioning techniques. 4. Demonstrated donning of sterile gloves.
Evaluation of Learning	1. Significant other is a slow learner. Indicates she understands but unable to repeat instructions. Has a sitter around the clock to support wife until more comfortable with situation. 2. Respiratory therapist (RT) is to instruct in ventilation.

Note: (B) Barriers
(E) Enhancements

Exhibit 13-1 Sample Teaching Plan: Ventilator-Dependent Patient

Patient's Name _____

Nursing Diagnosis	Learning Objective	Plan	Teaching Method*	Date Plan Established	Initials
Knowledge deficit related to sterile suctioning	The patient or family will demonstrate sterile suctioning.	Instruct in: 1. the need for sterile technique 2. appropriate equipment 3. technique of sterile suctioning.	1. L, G, D, R, P, M 2. L, D, P, M 3. L, D, R, P, C, M	3/11/87	E. J., R.N.
Knowledge deficit related to recognizing respiratory infection	The patient or family will identify the signs and symptoms of respiratory infection.	Instruct in the signs and symptoms of respiratory infection: 1. chills 2. fever 3. shortness of breath 4. productive cough.	L, P, M	3/11/87	E. J., R.N.
Knowledge deficit related to actions to be taken if patient has an obstructed airway	The patient or family will identify measures to be taken if airway becomes obstructed.	Instruct in: 1. signs and symptoms of obstructed airway 2. measures to take if airway obstructed: a. preoxygenate with ambu bag b. irrigate with normal saline if necessary c. suction patient d. if remains in distress call for emergency help.	1. L, P, M 2. L, G, D, R, P, C, M	3/11/87	E. J., R.N.

*Method of teaching codes: L = lecture; G = group discussion; D = demonstration; R = role playing; P = programmed instruction; C = contracts; M = media.

Plan	1. Study written instruction. Allow to practice gloving next visit.
	2. Confer with RT on progress of teaching of ventilator. RT on call 24°/day for significant other to call if problems with ventilator occur. Sitter is CPR certified.
Instruction	1. Instructed in appropriate equipment and care of equipment.
	2. Demonstrated gloving again; step-by-step instruction.
Evaluation of Learning	1. Significant other asked numerous questions; required gloving demonstration × 3 before understood.
	2. Significant other gloved 6 times before accomplished without breaking sterile technique. Inconsistent in technique.
Plan	Observe gloving technique next visit. Left a pair of gloves for significant other to practice with.
Instruction	1. Demonstrated suctioning techniques; step-by-step procedure.
	2. Instructed in precautions to be aware of; written instructions left with significant other.
Evaluation of Learning	Significant other gloved × 3 before perfecting technique. Consistent enough to begin suctioning technique.
Plan	Allow significant other to practice suctioning on doll next visit.
Instruction	Instructed in suctioning techniques while significant other demonstrated on doll.

Evaluation of Learning	Significant other apprehensive about suctioning doll. Broke technique only once.
Plan	Allow significant other to suction patient next week.
Instruction	Instructed significant other in suctioning technique as she suctioned patient.
Evaluation of Learning	Significant other did very well suctioning patient. Became excited when patient gagged.
Plan	Begin instruction in ambu technique.

Nursing Diagnosis: Knowledge Deficit Related to Recognizing Respiratory Infection

Nursing Diagnosis Addressed	Knowledge deficit related to recognizing respiratory infection
Teaching Directed To	Significant other
Learning Enhancements/ Barriers	Same as previous visits
Method of Teaching	L, P, D (see Exhibit 13-1 for codes)
Instruction	Instructed on signs and symptoms of respiratory infections. Written instruction sheet left with significant other.
Evaluation of Learning	Significant other able to recite signs and symptoms of respiratory infection with some prompting.

Plan	Ask significant other to identify signs and symptoms of respiratory infection next visit.

Nursing Diagnosis: Knowledge Deficit Related to Actions to be Taken If Patient Has an Obstructed Airway

Nursing Diagnosis Addressed	Knowledge deficit related to actions to be taken if patient has an obstructed airway
Teaching Directed To	Significant other
Learning Enhancements/ Barriers	Same as previous visits
Method of Teaching	L, P, D (see Exhibit 13-1 for codes)
Instruction	Instructed in signs and symptoms of obstructed airway. Written instructions left with significant other.
Evaluation of Learning	Significant other appeared to comprehend. Able to recite three signs/symptoms of airway obstruction.
Plan	Begin instruction in measures to take if airway obstructed.
Instruction	Demonstrated ambu bag techniques on doll. Allowed significant other to practice. Written instructions left with significant other.
Evaluation of Learning	Significant other is becoming more confident and comprehending faster. Becoming more accustomed to having patient home with ventilator.

Plan	Left doll for significant other to practice. Sitter to assist significant other in technique.
Instruction	Instructed in irrigation with normal saline if necessary. Written instructions left with significant other.
Evaluation of Learning	1. Significant other has comprehended suctioning techniques, ambu bag techniques. 2. Significant other demonstrated irrigation with normal saline and suctioning on doll. Accomplished procedure without incident.
Plan	1. Observe significant other irrigating with normal saline and suctioning on doll. 2. Reduce visits to 3× week and continue teaching as plan is revised due to patient's and significant other's needs.

NOTES

1. K. Daley and P. Perez, "Your Ventilator Patient *Can* Go Home Again," *Nursing,* December 1986, pp. 54–46.
2. R. Biovannoni, "Chronic Ventilator Care: From Hospital to Home," *Respiratory Therapy,* July/August 1984, p. 28.
3. Ibid., pp. 29–33.
4. Ibid., p. 29.
5. J. O'Ryan, "An Overview of Mechanical Ventilation in the Home," *Respiratory Management,* March/April 1987, pp. 27–34.

BIBLIOGRAPHY

Benvenuti, C.S. "Independence for the Quadriplegic: The Bantam Respirator." *American Journal of Nursing* (May 1979):918–920.

Carpenito, L. *Nursing Diagnosis: Application to Clinical Practice.* Philadelphia: J.B. Lippincott Co., 1983.

Carroll, P.F. *When Your Patient Must Depend on a Machine."* RN 12, no. 49 (December 1986): 14–15.

Castaldo, P. "Respiratory Home Care from the DME Point of View." *Home Healthcare Nurse* 2, no. 3 (March-April 1985):32–35.

Ciranowicz, M., Furan, C., Kupnick, S., Weiner, S., and Welsh, N. *Patient Teaching Manual 1.* Springhouse, Penn.: Springhouse Corp., 1987.

Clough, P., Lindenauer, D., Hayes, M., and Zekany, B. "Guidelines for Routine Respiratory Care of Patients with Spinal Cord Injury: A Clinical Report." *Physical Therapy* 9, no. 66 (September 1986):1395–1402.

Daley, K., and Perez, P. "Your Ventilator Patient Can Go Home Again." *Nursing*, December 1986, pp. 54–56.

Doenges, M. *Nursing Care Plans: Nursing Diagnosis in Planning Patient Care.* Philadelphia: F.A. Davis Co., 1984.

Fox, J. "Chronic Respiratory Patients: A New Challenge for Home Health Nursing." *Home Health Healthcare Nurse* 2, no. 3 (March-April 1985):13–16.

Frace, R. "Home Ventilation: An Alternative To Institutionalization." *Focus On Critical Care* 13, no. 6 (December 1986):28–34.

Gilmartin, M.E., et al. "Mechanical Ventilation in the Home: A New Mandate." *Respiratory Care* 5, no. 31 (May 1986):406–412.

Giovannoni, R. "Chronic Ventilator Care: From Hospital to Home." *Respiratory Therapy,* July/August 1984, pp. 29–33.

Goldberg, A. "Home Care for Life-Supported Persons: Is a National Approach the Answer?" *Chest,* November 1986, pp. 744–748.

Gould, J.E., and Wargo, J. *Home Health Nursing Care Plans.* Rockville, Md.: Aspen Publishers, Inc., 1987.

Jaffe, M., and Skidmore-Roth, L. *Medical-Surgical Nursing Care Plans.* Norwalk, Conn.: Appleton-Century-Crofts, 1986.

Kacmarek, R.M., et al. "Equipment Used for Ventilatory Support in the Home." *Respiratory Care* 4, no. 31 (April 1986):311–328.

Kopacz, M.A., and Moriartz-Wright, R. "Multidisciplinary Approach for the Patient on a Home Ventilator." *Heart & Lung* 3, no. 13 (May 1984):255–262.

Luckmann, J., and Sorensen, K. *Medical-Surgical Nursing: A Psychophysiologic Approach,* 2nd ed. Philadelphia: W.B. Saunders Co., 1980.

"Mechanical Ventilation at Home." *Emergency Medicine,* September 1985, pp. 44, 47.

McDonald, G.J. "A Home Care Program for Patients with Chronic Lung Disease." *Nursing Clinics of North America* 2, no. 16 (1981):259–273.

Neal, M., Cohen, P., and Cooper, P. *Nursing Care Planning Guides for Long-Term Care.* Monterey, Calif.: Wadsworth Health Sciences & Pacific Palisades, Calif.: NURSECO, Inc., 1981.

O'Ryan, J. "An Overview of Mechanical Ventilation in the Home." *Respiratory Management,* March/April 1987, pp. 27–34.

Phipps, W., Long, B., and Woods, N., eds. *Medical-Surgical Nursing: Concepts and Clinical Practice.* St. Louis: C.V. Mosby Co., 1987.

Pierson, D.J., and George, R.B. "Mechanical Ventilation in the Home: Possibilities and Prerequisites." *Respiratory Care* 31, no. 4 (April 1986):266–270.

Prentice, W.S. "Placement Alternatives for Long-Term Ventilator Care." *Respiratory Care* 31, no. 4 (April 1986):288–293.

Thompson, J., McFarland, G., Hirsch, J., Tucker, S., and Bowers, A. *Clinical Nursing.* St. Louis: C.V. Mosby Co., 1986.

Ulrich, S., Canale, S., and Wendell, S. *Nursing Care Planning Guides: A Nursing Diagnosis Approach.* Philadelphia: W.B. Saunders Co., 1986.

Appendix A

Glossary

Affective Domain	One of three domains: concerns learning behaviors dealing with expression of feelings, interests, attitudes, values, and appreciation.
Appeal	An attempt to overturn an unfavorable claims determination (denial).
Assessment	A systematic collection of data that assists one in identifying the needs, preferences, and abilities of a patient.
Caregiver	Person directly responsible for the patient's care.
Cognitive Domain	One of three domains: concerns learning behaviors dealing with intellectual ability.
Compliance	Cooperation and participation in the prescribed therapeutic regimen by the patient.
Coverage	Meets criteria for payment of services under the insurance benefit plan.
Coverage Compliance Review	Onsite compliance audit by fiscal intermediary to determine if payment of claims was appropriate.

Defining Characteristics	Signs and symptoms identified to describe various states of health.
Denial	Nonpayment of services rendered.
Diagnosis-Related Group	(DRG): Classification method that assigns general acute hospital inpatients into groups.
Diagnostic Category	Classification used to describe various states of health that the nurse can treat.
Educational Need	Need that can be satisfied by a learning experience.
Etiological and Contributing Factors	Those physiological, situational, and maturational factors that can cause a problem or influence its development.
Fiscal Intermediary	Private insurance company contracted by HCFA to administer the Medicare insurance program.
Goal	An aim or end toward which intervention is directed.
HCFA	Health Care Financing Administration. A department of the U.S. Department of Health and Human Services that administers the Medicare program.
Health Belief Model	Model developed to predict preventative health behaviors.
HIM-11	*Medicare Home Health Agency Manual* (HCFA Publication no. 11).
HIM-13.3	*Medicare Intermediary Manual* (HCFA Publication no. 13.3).
Insurance Carrier	Insurance companies with which HCFA contracts to administer Part B Medicare programs.
Knowledge Deficit	State in which the individual experiences a deficiency in cognitive knowledge or psychomotor skills that alter health maintenance.

Learning	Process of acquiring new knowledge, skills, or attitudes that are synthesized to produce behavior change in the individual.
Length of Stay	Phrase used when discussing how long a patient with a particular diagnosis stays in a care setting.
Medical Regimen	Therapeutic measures prescribed for patients by physicians and directed toward management or cure of illness or disease.
Medical Review	Prepayment review process by fiscal intermediary or private insurance company to determine payment or nonpayment of services rendered.
Medicare Beneficiary	Person eligible for Medicare benefits due to either age or disability.
Medicare Certified	Provider of services who meets the ten conditions of participation in the Medicare program.
Medicare Part A	Hospital insurance. Medical coverage available to almost everyone who is age 65 or over, disabled, or who has chronic renal disease.
Medicare Part B	Supplementary medical insurance. A voluntary program for which the Medicare beneficiary may decline coverage. Covers physician services and outpatient services.
Motivation	That which stimulates one toward action or inaction.
• **Extrinsic**	Forces outside the individual that cause one to act: rewards, punishments, changes in health, and life style.
• **Intrinsic**	Forces within the individual that cause one to act: values, beliefs, attitudes, unmet needs, and emotions.
NANDA	North American Nursing Diagnosis Association: a group composed of nurses from all regions of the United States and Canada

who are responsible for the development of the diagnostic classification system.

Nonpresumptive Status Denial rate one calendar quarter in excess of 2.5 percent; coverage compliance review denial rate in excess of 5 percent.

Nursing Diagnosis A statement that describes a health state or an actual or potential alteration in one's life process that nurses can treat in their practice domain.

Nursing Process Problem solving used in nursing practice: includes assessment, diagnosis, planning, implementation, and evaluation.

Objective Statement of intended outcomes or results to be achieved by the patient.

Patient Teaching Imparting of information to a patient.

PIP (Periodic Interim Payment) Reimbursement for an estimated number of visits. See HIM-15, Section 2407.

Postpayment Review Review by fiscal intermediary to determine if information submitted on HCFA 485, 486, and 487 is reflected in medical record.

PRECEDE Model Health education model that identifies certain factors in one's environment.

Presumptive Status Same as waiver of liability.

Psychomotor Domain One of three domains: covers learning behaviors dealing with skills known as motor skills.

Readiness To Learn The state of being both willing and able to make use of instruction.

Regional Intermediaries Ten fiscal intermediaries established by HCFA in an effort to standardize medical review of Medicare Part A claims.

Reimbursement Payment for services provided.

Reopened Claims A request to the fiscal intermediary to review its claim determination in a particular case; fiscal intermediary may reopen a case due to clerical error or good cause and reverse the initial claim determination.

Retroactive Denials Denials made after the claim has been paid.

Self-Care The personal and medical care performed by the patient.

Significant Other Person directly responsible for patient care.

Skilled Care Services that require the knowledge and skills of a professional to perform or teach.

Teaching/Learning Process Process in which knowledge, attitudes, and skills are imparted to and integrated by the learner.

Teaching Situation Includes the physical, interpersonal, and external environment.

Team Conference Interdisciplinary case conference where all disciplines involved in a patient's care meet to evaluate and revise the plan of care.

Appendix B

NANDA List of Nursing Diagnoses (Accepted Diagnoses from the Sixth National Conference, 1986)*

Activity Intolerance
Adjustment, Impaired
Airway Clearance, Ineffective
Anxiety

Body Temperature, Potential
  Alteration in
Bowel Elimination, Alterations in:
  Constipation
Bowel Elimination, Alterations in:
  Diarrhea
Bowel Elimination, Alterations in:
  Incontinence
Breathing Patterns, Ineffective

Cardiac Output, Alterations in:
  Decreased
Comfort, Alterations in: Pain
Comfort, Altered; Chronic Pain
Communication, Impaired Verbal

Coping, Ineffective Individual
Coping, Ineffective Family:
  Compromised
Coping, Ineffective Family:
  Disabling

Diversional Activity Deficit

Family Processes, Alterations in
Fear (specify)
Fluid Volume Deficit, Actual
Fluid Volume Deficit, Potential
Fluid Volume Excess

Gas Exchange, Impaired
Grieving, Anticipatory
Grieving, Dysfunctional
Growth and Development,
  Altered

*Reprinted with permission of North American Nursing Diagnosis Association, St. Louis University Department of Nursing, St. Louis, Missouri.

Health Maintenance, Alterations in
Home Maintenance Management,
 Impaired
Hopelessness
Hyperthermia
Hypothermia

Incontinence, Functional
Incontinence, Reflex
Incontinence, Stress
Incontinence, Total
Incontinence, Urge
Infection, Potential for
Injury, Potential for (specify)
 Poisoning
 Suffocation
 Trauma

Knowledge Deficit (specify)

Mobility, Impaired Physical

Noncompliance (specify)
Nutrition, Alterations in: Less
 Than Body Requirements
Nutrition, Alterations in: More
 Than Body Requirements
Nutrition, Alterations in: Potential
 for More Than Body
 Requirements

Oral Mucous Membrane,
 Alterations in

Parenting, Alterations in: Actual
Parenting, Alterations in:
 Potential

Post-trauma Response
Powerlessness

Rape Trauma Syndrome
Respiratory Functions, Alterations
 in: Airway Clearance
  Ineffective Breathing Patterns
  Ineffective Gas Exchange,
  Impaired

Self-Care Deficit: Total
 Feeding
 Bathing/Hygiene
 Dressing/Grooming
 Toileting
Self-Concept, Disturbance in
Sensory-Perceptual Alterations:
 Visual
 Auditory
 Kinesthetic
 Gustatory
 Tactile
 Olfactory
Sexual Dysfunction
Sexuality Patterns, Altered
Skin Integrity, Impairment of,
 Actual
Skin Integrity, Impairment of,
 Potential
Sleep Pattern Disturbance
Social Interaction, Impaired
Social Isolation
Spiritual Distress
Swallowing, Impaired

Thermoregulation, Ineffective
Thought Processes, Alterations in
Unilateral Neglect

Tissue Perfusion, Alteration in:
  Cardiopulmonary
  Cerebral
  Gastrointestinal
  Peripheral
  Renal

Urinary Elimination, Alteration in
  Patterns of
Urinary Retention

Violence, Potential for

Appendix C

Assessment, Teaching, and Documentation Tools

TEACHING ASSESSMENT GUIDE

Patient's Name _____

Primary Medical Diagnosis _____ Date of Onset _____

Secondary Medical Diagnosis _____ Date of Onset _____

Services Provided: __ SKN __ PT __ ST __ OT __ MSW __ HHA

I. Assessment of Learner
   A. Educational needs
      1. Normal body functions
      2. Health problems
      3. Medical regimen
      4. Preventative/health promotion measures
      5. Resources
   B. Educational abilities
      1. Readiness
      2. Attitude/motivation
      3. Background
         (a) medical
         (b) social
         (c) cultural
         (d) educational

II. Teacher Situation
    A. Physical environment (where teaching takes place): describe enhancements/barriers to learning
    B. Interpersonal environment
        1. Patient/teacher relationship
        2. Patient/family relationship
    C. External environment
        1. Resources
        2. Support
III. Nursing Diagnosis
    A. Identification of problem
    B. Nursing diagnosis statement

TEACHING PLAN

Patient's Name: _____

Nursing Diagnosis	Learning Objectives	Teaching Plan	Teaching Method*	Date Plan Established	Initials

*Method of teaching codes: L = lecture; G = group discussion; D = demonstration; R = role playing; P = programmed instruction; C = contracts; M = media.

DOCUMENTATION TOOL

Date	Nursing Diagnosis Addressed	Teaching Directed To	Learning Enhancements/ Barriers	Teaching Method	Instruction	Evaluation of Learning	Plan	Initials

Appendix D

HCFA Manuals*

The following HCFA manuals are available for purchase through the National Technical Information Service. If you wish to purchase any of these manuals, call either (703) 487-4630 or toll free (800) 336-4700 to ascertain the current price and receive purchasing instructions. Specify the report number, publication number, and title of the desired item when contacting NTIS.

Report No.	Pub. No.	Title
PB85-950099	HCFA Pub. 7	State Operation Manual
PB85-950199	HCFA Pub. 9	Outpatient Physical Therapy Provider Manual
PB85-950299	HCFA Pub. 13-1	Part A Intermediary Manual
PB85-950399	HCFA Pub. 13-2	Part A Intermediary Manual, Part 2: Audits, Reimbursement, Program Administration
PB85-959499	HCFA Pub. 13-4	Part A Intermediary Manual, Part 4: Audit Procedures
PB85-959599	HCFA Pub. 14-1	Medicare Carriers Manual, Part 1: Fiscal Administration

*Information obtained from National Technical Information Service, U.S. Department of Commerce, Springfield, Virginia.

Report No.	Pub. No.	Title
PB85-950699	HCFA Pub. 14-2	Medicare Carriers Manual, Part 2: Program Administration
PB85-959799	HCFA Pub. 15-1 (Chapter 27)	Provider Reimbursement Manual, Part I: Reimbursement for ESRD Service and Supplies
PB85-950899	HCFA Pub. 15-II-A	Provider Reimbursement Manual, Part II: General
PB85-950999	HCFA Pub. 15-II-C	Provide Reimbursement Manual, Part II: Cost Report for Skilled Nursing Facility Complexes
PB85-951099	HCFA Pub. 15-II-D	Provider Reimbursement Manual, Part II: Cost Report for Home Health Agencies
PB85-951199	HCFA Pub. 15-II-F	Provider Reimbursement Manual, Part II: Cost Report for Outpatient Physical Therapy and Speech Pathology Providers
PB85-951299	HCFA Pub. 15-II-G	Provider Reimbursement Manual, Part II: Cost Reporting for Providers with All-Inclusive Rate or No-Charge Structures
PB85-951399	HCFA Pub. 15-2-I	Provider Reimbursement Manual, Part II: Independent Renal Dialysis Facility Cost Report
PB85-951499	HCFA Pub. 15-II-J	Provider Reimbursement Manual, Part II: Cost Reports for Home Office
PB85-951599	HCFA Pub. 15-II-L	Provider Reimbursement Manual, Part II: Provider Cost Reports for Hospital and Hospital Health Care Complex, HCFA-2552-83
PB85-953699	HCFA Pub. 15-II-N	Provider Reimbursement Manual, Part II: Cost Reporting for Hospice

Report No.	Pub. No.	Title
PB85-953799	HCFA Pub. 15-II-O	Provider Reimbursement Manual, Part II: Cost Reporting for Hospital and Hospital Health Care Complex, HCFA-2552-84
PB85-954199	HCFA Pub. 15-II-S	Provider Reimbursement Manual, Part II: Cost Report for Hospital and Hospital Health Care Complex, HCFA-2552-85
PB85-954099	HCFA Pub. 19	Peer Review Organization Manual
PB85-951799	HCFA Pub. 21	Hospice Manual
PB85-951899	HCFA Pub. 23-1	HCFA Regional Office Manual, Part 1: General
PB85-951999	HCFA Pub. 23-2	HCFA Regional Office Manual, Part 2: Medicare
PB85-952099	HCFA Pub. 23-3	HCFA Regional Office Manual, Part 3: Program Integrity
PB85-952199	HCFA Pub. 23-4	HCFA Regional Office Manual, Part 4: Standards and Certifications Guidelines
PB85-952299	HCFA Pub. 23-6	HCFA Regional Office Manual, Part 6: Medicaid
PB85-953999	HCFA Pub. 27	Medicare Rural Health Clinic Manual
PB85-953599	HCFA Pub. 29	Medicare Renal Dialysis Facility Manual
PB85-952399	HCFA Pub. 45-2	State Medicaid Manual, Part 2: State Organization
PB85-952499	HCFA Pub. 45-3	State Medicaid Manual, Part 3: Eligibility
PB85-952599	HCFA Pub. 45-4	State Medicaid Manual, Part 4: Services
PB85-952699	HCFA Pub. 45-5	State Medicaid Manual, Part 5: Early and Periodic Screening, Diagnosis and Treatment

Report No.	Pub. No.	Title
PB85-952799	HCFA Pub. 45-6	State Medicaid Manual, Part 6: Payment for Service
PB85-952899	HCFA Pub. 45-7	State Medicaid Manual, Part 7: Quality Control
PB85-952999	HCFA Pub. 45-8	State Medicaid Manual, Part 8: Program Integrity
PB85-953099	HCFA Pub. 45-9	State Medicaid Manual, Part 9: Utilization Control
PB85-953199	HCFA Pub. 45-11	State Medicaid Manual, Part 11: Medicaid Management Information System
PB85-953299	HCFA Pub. 45-13	State Medicaid Manual, Part 14: Administrative
PB85-953499	HCFA Pub. 45-14	State Medicaid Manual, Part 14: Administrative
PB85-953499	HCFA Pub. 45-15	State Medicaid Manual, Part 15: Medicaid Eligibility Determination and Information Retrieval System
PB85-953899	HCFA Pub. 75	Health Maintenance Organization/Competitive Medical Plan Manual

*   *   *   *

The following manuals are available for purchase through the Government Printing Office (GPO). If you wish to purchase any of these manuals, call (202) 275-3050 to determine the current price and receive purchasing instructions. Specify the Subscription Title S/N and the List ID of the item(s) requested.

A subscription includes the basic manual and all revisions for approximately 1 year. When placing telephone orders (current GPO prepaid deposit account, Visa, or Master Charge), call (202) 783-3238. When answered, give the operator the Subscription Title S/N, the List ID, and your account number. The number of the complaint desk is (202) 275-3054.

Manual Title/Pub. No.	List ID	Subscription Title S/N
Coverage Issues Manual HCFA Pub. 6	MCIA	917-012-00000-8
Hospital Manual HCFA Pub. 10	HMP	917-005-00000-1
Home Health Agency Manual HCFA Pub. 11	HHAM	917-004-00000-5
Skilled Nursing Facility Manual HCFA Pub. 12	SNFM	917-008-00000-1
Provider Reimbursement Manual HCFA Pub. 15-1	PRM	917-007-00000-4
Medicare Intermediary Manual, Part 3: Claims Process HCFA Pub. 13-3	MIMA	917-006-00000-8
Medicare Carriers Manual, Part 3: Claims Process HCFA Pub. 14-3	MCMB	917-003-00000-9

Appendix E

Resources for Teaching Materials

AUDIOVISUAL RESOURCES

Audiovisual Resources for Hypertension Education (1984)
Learning Resource Center
University of Michigan Medical School
1135 East Catherine
Box 38
Ann Arbor, MI 48109

Locating Audiovisual Materials
National Health Information Clearinghouse
P.O. Box 1133
Washington, DC 20013-1133

Milner-Fenwick, Inc.
2125 Greenspring Drive
Timonium, MD 21093

Recommended Audiovisual Resources for Diabetes Education (1984)
Michigan Diabetes Research and Training Center and the Department
    of Postgraduate Medicine and Health Professions Education
University of Michigan Medical School
Ann Arbor, MI 48109

ORGANIZATIONS

National Organizations

American Academy of Pediatrics
141 Northwest Point
Elk Grove Village, IL 60007

American Association of Diabetes Educators
500 North Michigan Avenue, Suite 1400
Chicago, IL 60611

American Association of Retired Persons
510 King Street
Alexandria, VA 22314

American Cancer Society
Public and Professional Education Depts.
90 Park Avenue
New York, NY 10016

American Diabetes Association
2 Park Avenue
New York, NY 10016

American Heart Association
7320 Greenville Avenue
Dallas, TX 75231

American Lung Association
1740 Broadway
New York, NY 10019

Association for the Care of Children's Health
3615 Wisconsin Avenue, N.W.
Washington, DC 20016

Council of Home Health Agencies and Community Health Services
National League for Nursing
10 Columbus Circle, 24th Floor
New York, NY 10019

Juvenile Diabetes Foundation International
23 East 26th Street
New York, NY 10010

National Association for Home Care
519 C Street, N.E.
Washington, DC 20002

National Council on Patient Information and Education
1625 I Street, N.W., Suite 1010
Washington, DC 20006

National Home Caring Council
Homemaker/Home Health Aide Accreditation
235 Park Avenue South
New York, NY 10003

National Hospice Organization
1901 North Fort Myer Drive, Suite 402
Arlington, VA 22209

National Society for Medical Research
1000 Vermont Avenue
Washington, DC 20005

Oncology Nursing Society
3111 Banksville Road
Pittsburgh, PA 15216

Society for Public Health Education
703 Market Street
San Francisco, CA 94103

United Cancer Council, Inc.
1803 North Meridian Street
Indianapolis, IN 46202

Support/Self-Help Groups

Association of Heart Patients, Inc.
P.O. Box 54305
Atlanta, GA 30308

Candlelighters Foundation
2025 Eye Street, N.W., Suite 1011
Washington, DC 20006

The Coronary Club, Inc.
3659 Green Road, Room 200
Cleveland, OH 44122

The Mended Hearts, Inc.
7320 Greenville Avenue
Dallas, TX 75231

United Ostomy Association, Inc.
2001 West Beverly Boulevard
Los Angeles, CA 90057

PUBLICATIONS

Bibliography

The Child and Health Care: A Bibliography
Washington, D.C.: Association for the Care of Children's Health, 1983.

Books/Booklets

Adult Patient Education in Cancer
Bethesda, Md.: U.S. Dept. of Health and Human Services, NIH, 1982.

About Your High Blood Pressure Medicines
Rockville, Md.: U.S. Pharmacopeial Convention, 1981.

An Easier Way: Handbook for Elderly and Handicapped
Jean V. Sargent
New York: Walker & Co., 1982.

The Breast Cancer Digest: A Guide to Medical Care, Emotional Support,
    Educational Programs and Resources, 2nd ed.
Bethesda, Md.: National Cancer Institute (NIH Pub. No. 84-1691),
    1984.

Cancer Care: A Guide for Patient Education
Marilee Donovan
New York: Appleton-Century-Crofts, 1981.

Cardiac Rehabilitation: A Comprehensive Nursing Approach
Patricia M. Comoss et al.
Philadelphia: J.B. Lippincott Co., 1979.

The Complete Book of Medical Tests
Mark Moskowitz and Michael Osband
New York: W.W. Norton & Co., 1984.

Coping with Cancer: A Resource for the Health Professional
B. Blumberg et al.
Bethesda, Md.: National Cancer Institute (NIH Pub. No. 80-2080),
    1980.

Diabetes and Patient Education: A Daily Nursing Challenge
A. Van Son
New York: Appleton-Century-Crofts, 1982.

Diet and Nutrition: A Resource for Parents of Children with Cancer
National Cancer Institute
Cancer Information Clearinghouse
Building 31, Room 10-A-18
Bethesda, MD 20205

Educating Diabetic Patients
G. Steiner and P. Lawrence, eds.
New York: Springer Publishing Co., 1981.

*Educational Materials for and About Young People with Diabetes: Selected
Annotations* (1983)
National Diabetes Information Clearinghouse
Box NDIC
Bethesda, MD 20205

Effective Patient Education: A Guide to Increased Compliance
Donna R. Falvo
Rockville, Md.: Aspen Publishers, Inc., 1985.

The Essential Guide to Prescription Drugs
James W. Long
Scranton, PA: Harper & Row, 1982.

Health Education Planning: A Diagnostic Approach
Lawrence W. Green et al.
Palo Alto, Calif.: Mayfield Publishing, 1980.

Help Yourself: Tips for Teenagers with Cancer
National Cancer Institute
Cancer Information Clearinghouse
Building 31, Room 10-A-18
Bethesda, MD 20205

Hypertension Care: A Guide for Patient Education
Shirley Mason, ed.
New York: Appleton-Century-Crofts, 1982.

Medication Teaching Manual: A Guide for Patient Counseling
Bethesda, Md.: American Society of Hospital Pharmacists, 1983.

Outcome Standards for Cancer Patient Education
Oncology Nursing Society
3111 Banksville Road
Pittsburgh, PA 15216

Patient and Family Education, Tools, Techniques, and Theory
Rose-Marie Duda McCormick and Tmar Gilson-Parkevish
New York: Wiley Medical Publications, 1979.

Patient Education: Issues, Principles, and Guidelines
Sally H. Ranking and Karen L. Duffy
Philadelphia: J.B. Lippincott, 1983.

Preparing Children and Families for Health Care Encounters
Washington, D.C.: Association for the Care of Children's Health, 1980.

*The Prevention and Treatment of Five Complications of Diabetes: A Guide for
    Primary Care Practitioners*
Bethesda, Md.: National Diabetes Advisory Board, Centers for Disease
    Control, 1983.

The Process of Patient Education
Barbara K. Redman
St. Louis: C.V. Mosby, 1984.

Staff Manual for Teaching Patients About Diabetes Mellitus
Jean E. Espenshade
Chicago: American Hospital Association, 1982.

Understanding Your Medications
Washington, D.C.: National Health Information Clearinghouse, 1983.

Catalogs/Lists

Audiovisual Resources for Hypertension Education (1984)
Learning Resource Center
University of Michigan Medical School
1135 East Catherine
Box 38
Ann Arbor, MI 48109

Publications Catalog (1984)
American Academy of Pediatrics
141 Northwest Point
Elk Grove Village, IL 60007

Recommended Audiovisual Resources for Diabetes Education (1984)
Michigan Diabetes Research and Training Center and the Department
　　of Postgraduate Medicine and Health Professions Education
University of Michigan Medical School
Ann Arbor, MI 48109

Source Book for Health Education: Materials and Community Resources
Superintendent of Documents
U.S. Government Printing Office
Washington, DC 20402

Sources
Pharmaceutical Manufacturers Association
1100 15th Street, N.W.
Washington, DC 20005

Patient Medication Information Sheets

American Association of Retired Persons
Pharmacy Service
510 King Street
Alexandria, VA 22314

Drug Use Education Tips (DUET)
1984 U.S.P. *Advice for the Patient*
12601 Twinbrook Parkway
Rockville, MD 20852

Periodicals

Cardiovascular Nursing Journal
American Heart Association
7320 Greenville Avenue
Dallas, TX 75231

Caring
National Association for Home Care
519 C Street, N.E.
Washington, DC 20002

Current Awareness in Health Education
Bureau of Health Education
Centers for Disease Control
Building 14
Atlanta, GA 30333

Diagnosis
Medical Economics, Inc.
680 Kinderkamack Road
Oradell, NJ 07649

Health Education Quarterly
Society for Public Health Education
703 Market Street
San Francisco, CA 94103

Heart & Lung
C.V. Mosby Co.
11830 Westline Industrial Drive
St. Louis, MO 63146

Orthopaedic Nursing
"An Efficient Patient Teaching Tool," 2, no. 1 (January/February 1983).
"The Nurse as Educator," 2, no. 4 (July/August 1983).

Patient Education and Counseling
Excerpta Medica
P.O. Box 3085
Princeton, NJ 08540

Patient Education Newsletter
Division of Health Education–Health Behaviors
School of Public Health
University of Alabama in Birmingham
930 South 20th Street
Birmingham, AL 35294

Pediatrics
"Pediatric Patient Education: Challenge for the '80s," 74, no. 5 (Suppl.)
    (November 1984).

Respiratory Therapy
Barrington Publications, Inc.
8825 South Barrington Avenue
Los Angeles, CA 90049

OTHER RESOURCES

Center for Health Promotion and Education
Centers for Disease Control
Building 3, Room 117
1600 Clifton Road, N.E.
Atlanta, GA 30333

Channing L. Bete Co., Inc.
200 State Road
South Deerfield, MA 01373
(Booklets and brochures)

Consumer Health Information Corp.
Watergate 600, Suite 720
600 New Hampshire Avenue, N.W.
Washington, DC 20037

Eli Lilly & Co.
307 East McCarty Street
P.O. Box 618
Indianapolis, IN 46285

Fleischman's Margarine
625 Madison Avenue
New York, NY 10022

Food and Drug Administration
Office of Consumer and Professional Relations
Center for Drugs and Biologics
5600 Fishers Lane (HFN-10)
Rockville, MD 20857

High Blood Pressure Information Center
120/80 National Institutes of Health
Bethesda, MD 20205

Joint Commission on Accreditation of Healthcare Organizations
875 North Michigan Avenue
Chicago, IL 60611

Medcom Inc.
1633 Broadway
New York, NY 10019

Medfact, Inc.
1112 Andrew, N.E.
Massilon, OH 44645

Media Medica, Inc.
East Hanover, NJ 07936

National Cancer Institute
Cancer Information Clearinghouse
Building 31, Room 10-A-18
Bethesda, MD 20205

National Center for Health Education
30 East 29th Street
New York, NY 10016

National Diabetes Information Clearinghouse
Box NDIC
Bethesda, MD 20205

National Health Information Clearinghouse
P.O. Box 1133
Washington, DC 20013-1133

National Heart, Lung and Blood Institute
Office of Information
9000 Rockville Pike
Bethesda, MD 20205

National Rehabilitation Information Center
4407 Eighth Street, N.E.
Washington, DC 20017

Office of Health Maintenance Organizations
Department of Health and Human Services
5600 Fishers Lane
Rockville, MD 20857

Warner/Chilcott Laboratories
Division of Parke-Davis
201 Tabor Road
Morris Plains, NJ 07950

Appendix F

Ten Regional Intermediaries

HCFA designated ten intermediaries to service freestanding home health agencies in the indicated states, the District of Columbia, Puerto Rico, and the Virgin Islands as follows:

1. **Aetna Life and Casualty:** Alabama, Florida, Georgia, and Mississippi
2. **Associated Hospital Service of Maine:** Connecticut, Maine, Massachusetts, New Hampshire, Rhode Island, and Vermont
3. **Blue Cross and Blue Shield of South Carolina:** Kentucky, North Carolina, South Carolina, and Tennessee
4. **Blue Cross and Blue Shield United of Wisconsin:** Michigan, Minnesota, and Wisconsin
5. **Blue Cross of California:** Alaska, Arizona, California, Hawaii, Idaho, Nevada, Oregon, and Washington
6. **Blue Cross of Greater Philadelphia:** Delaware, District of Columbia, Maryland, Pennsylvania, Virginia, and West Virginia
7. **Blue Cross of Iowa, Inc.:** Colorado, Iowa, Kansas, Missouri, Montana, Nebraska, North Dakota, South Dakota, Utah, and Wyoming
8. **Health Care Service Corporation** (Chicago, Illinois): Illinois, Indiana, and Ohio
9. **New Mexico Blue Cross and Blue Shield, Inc.:** Arkansas, Louisiana, New Mexico, Oklahoma, and Texas
10. **The Prudential Insurance Company of America:** New Jersey, New York, Puerto Rico, and the Virgin Islands

Index

235

About the Authors

Janet E. Jackson, BSN, MS, is an assistant professor at the University of Arkansas, a part-time coronary care unit staff nurse at the Washington Regional Medical Center in Fayetteville, and former agency director of the Washington County Visiting Nurses Association. She is a member of the American Nurses' Association, the American Association of Critical Care Nurses and Sigma Theta Tau. Ms. Jackson has frequently contributed articles to the *Home Health Journal*.

Elizabeth A. Johnson, BSN, CNA, is Executive Director of Regional Health Systems, Inc. of Muskogee, Oklahoma. Ms. Johnson is a home health care consultant who has been working in the home care field for over eight years.